04/04/2023.

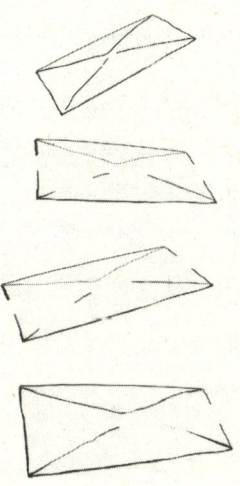

Missed Connections

A MEMOIR *in* LETTERS

NEVER SENT

BRIAN FRANCIS

MCCLELLAND & STEWART

Library and Archives Canada Cataloguing in Publication
data is available upon request.

ISBN: 978-0-7710-3814-3
ebook ISBN: 978-0-7710-3815-0

Book design by Lisa Jager
Jacket images by Lisa Jager
Typeset in Charter ITC Pro by M&S, Toronto
Printed in Canada

McClelland & Stewart,
a division of Penguin Random House Canada Limited,
a Penguin Random House Company
www.penguinrandomhouse.ca

1 2 3 4 5   25 24 23 22 21

Penguin
Random House
McCLELLAND & STEWART

For Susan and Wendy

CONTENTS

INTRODUCTION 1

INTRODUCTION

In 1992, I placed a personal ad in the newspaper.

I was twenty-one years old and had just started my third year of university. For any Generation Z readers, 1992 was important historically as it was the year that fire was invented.

It was also a year of pushing boundaries and challenging the establishment. Madonna came out with her book *Sex*. Sinéad O'Connor caused a maelstrom when she ripped up a photo of Pope John Paul II on *Saturday Night Live*. Charles and Diana officially announced their separation after years of scrutiny. And the tribute concert for Freddie Mercury, who had died from AIDS the previous year, was broadcast to a billion people worldwide. In addition, the World Health Organization declassified homosexuality as a mental illness.

In my corner of the world, in a mid-sized city in Southwestern Ontario, some other significant changes were taking place. I had just started the process of coming out. Not that the closet doors had flung wide open or anything. It was more of a gradual squeak, as these sorts of things tend to go. One of my sisters knew, as well as some of my high school friends. And the people I'd met via the local gay scene knew. But my parents didn't know. And the straight guys I shared a house with didn't know. So I was in a state of precarious balancing, one foot planted in secrecy and the other foot in honesty, straddling two worlds, not unlike many queer people in their early days of emergence.

My classified ad ran for three issues and cost sixty-five dollars, which was a lot of money for me, especially in those student days. I was perpetually broke. I ate sardine sandwiches. I smoked my cigarettes only halfway to make them last longer. I bought clothes on Friday, wore them to the bar on Saturday, and returned them on Monday. I was constantly on the phone to my parents asking for loans. The money I'd saved during the summer while working in Chemical Valley, in my hometown of Sarnia, Ontario, and which was to last me throughout the school year, had suddenly, and inexplicably, run low.

"But, Brian," my dad would say. "It's October."

As to why I would've sunk that kind of cash into a personal ad rather than spend the money on something more practical, like a new pirate shirt—this was the early nineties, after all—I can only explain my actions by saying that I was desperate for love. It was something I had never experienced. Lust, absolutely. Hurt—are you kidding me? But romantic love, and everything I imagined it would feel like, had eluded me. What I craved more than anything was security and reassurance, of being accepted. A connection. I wanted to see someone looking back at me and know that I was loved for who I was, not for whatever I'd been masquerading as up until that point in time.

In retrospect, I don't think I would have recognized Prince Charming even if he had come galloping along on a white horse with a box of Pot of Gold assorted chocolates tucked under his arm. What did I know about love at twenty-one? What *could* I have known, after having to grapple with the shame, fear, and suffocating isolation that came with growing up gay in a small city? I was surrounded by a brick wall, one that I'd been constructing since my childhood, although I didn't realize it. Nor did I realize how thick and high the wall was.

In spite of my feelings of wrongness, of never being good enough, or valued or equal, I still, somehow, believed in love. Specifically, gay love. "This desperation is raging," I wrote in my journal. "I'm clinging to scraps of hope."

But the ad was also about excitement. And adventure—I placed it to see what was possible. For so long, I'd kept gay men at a distance. It was a guilt-by-association thing. Now that I was coming into my own, now that I was starting to feel comfortable in my own skin, I became increasingly curious: Who was out there?

Before the advent of smart phones and dating apps, even before the internet, personal classified ads were one of the only outlets available for queer people to meet one another. Sure, there were bars, and bathhouses. And the grocery store, if you were expert at casting longing glances across the potatoes. But for many, particularly those who were closeted, personal ads were one of the few ways for queer people to connect. I had responded to a classified ad the year before I placed my own. I'd been a bundle of nerves, waiting to see if I'd get a response. (I never did.)

Knowing that I'd likely be in competition with other ads appearing in the same issue, I didn't approach the wording of my ad lightly. I'd need to stand out if I was going to snare the attention of Mr. Right. And sixty-five dollars was a fortune, after all. I could have used that money to pay off some of my debt (university students should never be allowed to register for a Petro-Canada credit card) or make a payment on the car I'd purchased a few months earlier. Or spend it on alcohol. So I had to ensure I got a return on my investment. Rather than write something predictable, like "Single gay male, brown hair and eyes, seeks same for special times and quiet nights," I opted to showcase my sparkling personality.

Gorgeous blond hunk, 6′2″, 200 lb of solid muscle— not! Real cute university student, 21, seeks same. Tired of narcissists and tired of being alone. Princess Di and Rambo wannabes need not apply.

I remember sitting at my large wooden desk in the basement of the student house where I lived, waiting for the moment when I'd be alone so I could call to place the ad without being overheard. It was impossible at times to keep anything private in that house, and the threat of exposure was constant. The receptionist on the other end remarked, "Oh, that's a good ad!" and I thought, "Yes, yes it is." If I could charm the newspaper's classifieds receptionist— someone who no doubt wrote down the wailings of the heartsick and lonely day in and day out—then the sky really was the limit.

A couple of days after my ad ran, I called the newspaper to inquire about the mountain of letters that were likely overtaking their office by that point.

"You've got four," I was told.

Four?!? How was that even possible? Had there been a Canada Post strike? Was there a typo in the box number? I had paid sixty-five dollars for four replies? But I reminded myself that all it would take was one letter from the right person. So I hopped into my 1982 shit-brown Mazda 626 (which I'd christened Mr. Feces) and booted it to the newspaper's office to collect my sparse offerings.

As I drove to the office, I wondered: What if this reaching out had been for nothing? I had finally tried to connect with someone, but I had never considered that no one might want to connect with me. What if I was more alone than I realized? What if I walked away from this experiment even lonelier than I had been going into it?

What if there truly was no one for me?

When I called the newspaper again a few days later, I was relieved to hear there were more envelopes, and a few more the next time. When all was said and done, I received around twenty-five responses. Maybe not the landslide I had hoped for, but it was twenty-five more chances at love than I'd had before I placed the ad.

I'd resist the urge to open the letters right then and there in the newspaper office parking lot and instead race home in Mr. Feces, a trail of exhaust following me as I tore through the streets, to barricade myself in my locked room and pore over the letters, as if each one were a sacred text. So much hope riding on a couple of paragraphs written by a stranger.

While it was fun to read the letters, to decode their subtexts and to imagine what the person looked like (only a few had included a photo), I was, admittedly, a little underwhelmed by the responses. There were some that I marked with a circle in the top left-hand corner of the envelope—an opening, a point of entry, of possibility. Others were given an x in the same spot and set aside. Too old, too boring, too humourless, too delusional.

I met with a handful of respondents. One for lunch. Another for drinks in a town thirty minutes away. I met one in a building on the university campus. And, with each encounter, I felt the same disappointment when I arrived on the scene. Not that any were unattractive or had sold themselves inauthentically, but I had very specific ideas as to what I was looking for, and I knew immediately if someone fit the bill or not. Or was it something else? Maybe it was easier to reject people before they could reject me.

So, no love connections. Not even any lacklustre sex. Sixty-five dollars down the drain, and the adventure, though a much-needed distraction for a couple of weeks, had got me nowhere. I was still single, semi-closeted, and just like my ad said, still "tired of being alone."

For some reason, I saved the letters I had dismissed, those envelopes with their tiny x's. I might have felt that throwing them out was a further rejection. These men had taken a chance, after all, a greater chance than I'd taken. They'd made themselves vulnerable to a stranger. They'd written into the void with the same hopes as me. And the void had answered with a resounding silence.

But I have a habit of hanging on to weird bits and pieces of my life—birthday cards, buttons, unflattering photos. I've always believed that the random and unfiltered souvenirs of our lives, rather than the curated and polished, are the most revealing.

I kept the letters in a cardboard box with other miscellaneous things: my high school yearbooks, elementary school Valentine cut-out cards, photo albums I made as a child that contained carefully peeled shreds of my sunburned skin. (Yes, I was a weird kid.) The boxes travelled with me over the years, and I didn't think much about the letters. But one winter day, a few years back, I rediscovered them. I tend to avoid digging through the boxes, mainly because it's a pain to haul everything out, but also because I have a habit of sinking into the past, sometimes giving it more weight than the present. It's such an easy trap, to take all your past experiences and package them up in a way that provides a tidy frame of perspective and structure, of narrative, in ways that the present can't. The past is always there, waiting. Even as I write this, each word I type on my screen immediately moves into the past.

On that particular winter day, I decided to indulge myself. I read those thirteen letters again, now more than a quarter-century old, the paper and envelopes yellowing, the handwritten and typed words fading. The letters seemed finite in a way they hadn't before. I seemed finite, too. I realized how much time had passed since these letters were written. These men had no idea who I was or that I still had their letters—letters that had been deposited into a mailbox almost thirty years ago, but could have blown away instead, floated through the air like tiny white sails.

These letters never even got the courtesy of a response.

Where were these thirteen men now? I wondered. No doubt some were dead, or elderly. But others, closer to my age, would still be alive, wouldn't they? Did they remember writing these letters? Where had their paths taken them? And had they ever found love?

Revisiting the letters at a much different stage in my life revealed their unique and awkward charms. I found myself asking, How might I reply to them now, writing not from the perspective of a wide-eyed youth but from the decidedly more wrinkled perspective of a man firmly at the midpoint of his life?

I considered my twenty-one-year-old self, someone who has become a little blurrier, less tangible, with each passing year. As I gallop towards middle age (truth be told, I'm there already, although it's hard for me to believe), I can't help but think of that twenty-one-year-old as a stranger, too. What would I say to him, the young man who was just coming out, who had gone in search of love and companionship?

Was it possible these strangers could help me connect to him as well, the person I used to be?

So I sat down and I did what I hadn't done twenty-nine years earlier.

I replied to those thirteen letters.

Letter 1

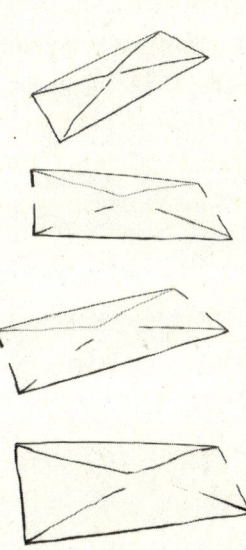

Hello "hunk"

Today is Sunday, Sept 27, and I grabbed a copy
of the newspaper on my way home from the gym.
I've glanced at the companion column before,
but your ad definitely got my attention. I've
read it a few times, but I'm still confused.
What part of the ad does the "not" refer to?
I'm 5 feet 11 inches and weigh in at 175 pounds.
I work out at least 3 times a week, sometimes
more, so I'm pretty solid. I get lots of
compliments, especially on my arms. I have
blond curly hair and brown eyes. I know some
people from the university but no one with your
description who would be up for some "guy fun."
Here are a couple of photos. They're not great.
The lighting is bad in one of them. But you'll
get a sense of what I look like. I bet you'll get
a lot of letters, but if you like what you see,
write back and maybe include a photo?
Hope to hear from you.

Dwayne

Dear Dwayne,

I knew who you were. I recognized you from your photos, bad lighting and all. I don't think we had ever spoken or inter- acted with one another, though. It was funny, how minus- cule the gay community in our university town could seem at times, how jam-packed the bar could get on a Saturday night, and yet there were people I never spoke to or whose paths I never crossed.

I rarely go to gay bars anymore. Not that I still can't, but I'm asleep by eleven thirty most Saturday nights. Still, I miss being twenty-one and roaring into the weekends with a vengeance. I'll hear a new Lady Gaga song and think, "I'd be fucking killing it on the dance floor right now." I miss the excitement and possibilities. The Saturday night people parade. When you're gay and not living in a metropolis like Toronto, there aren't many options when it comes to night- life. So you, and every other queer person, have no choice but to make do with whatever bars and watering holes there are, regardless of your interests or inclinations. But this, for me, was always the charm. Sure, big cities might boast more diverse entertainment offerings, permitting people to stay within the comfort of their cliques, but where is the joy in sameness? Give me a smoky room with no windows, volunteer DJs, and a spinning mirror ball dangling precariously from the ceiling. Give me dykes, drag queens, leather daddies, trans men and women, bears and twinks. Give me your closeted, your brazenly open, your flaming and your butch. Give me your old, young, fat, thin. Your messy drunks and your anal-retentive gay guys in pleated khakis. Put them all in the same space while "Rhythm Is a Dancer" thumps from a shitty sound system and you've got my brand of gay bar heaven.

And yet, as with everything in life, there was a flip side. The bar scene could feel stifling at times, an arena of competition and negativity. I wanted to be myself, but I still felt pressure to conform. I wanted freedom, but instead I was confined. I sought companionship but often walked away feeling lonelier than I had at the start of the night. The bar was where I sought solace, but instead I often felt judged. You'd be either praised or dismissed based on your looks, your body, your age, your clothing, whether your circle of friends was the "right" circle. There were few rituals I enjoyed more than getting ready to go out, but the pressure was always on to look hot, desirable. A piece of man candy. Those blessed with muscular bodies could get away with a simple white T-shirt and jeans—not an option for the rest of us mortals sucking in our stomachs and trying to cover up other imperfections with blazers or baggy pants. It was hard, at times, to see my reflection in the length of mirror along the dance floor and not feel deflated. Good looks and a hard body could get you anywhere on a Saturday night. Or so it seemed to me.

There I was, trying desperately to get laid, watching some muscle-bound guy saunter by. I'd pray for a look back, a signal of mutual attraction, but it rarely happened. I didn't have a chance. Not that rejection was unfamiliar to me. By that point, I was well versed in it—just not rejection by other gay men. And that subset of exclusion, the refusal by my own kind, was a particularly deep wound.

Now that I consider your letter, it was brave of you to include your photo. I wouldn't have done it. It would have made me feel too vulnerable, to know that I had sent a stranger a photo of myself. That the stranger might know who I was but I wouldn't know him. He could have shown the photo to his friends. I could just imagine being pointed out at the bar. *That's the loser over there! As if!!!"* Cue the cacophony of mean girl laughter.

No doubt you thought taking that risk would pay off. You did have a nice physique, after all.

But sadly, Dwayne, you just weren't my type. Muscular guys made me too self-conscious about my own body. I was a fat kid, you see. Over 200 pounds at thirteen years old. Specifically, 203 pounds. That number had been scorched into my brain when someone said it out loud. Weight's a funny thing. So long as no numbers are spoken, it's almost as if those numbers don't exist. There can be so much self-denial when it comes to weight. I don't mean your weight is something you can hide, although there are ways to camou-flage it. But you can't escape your body, your physicality. It's always there, surrounding you, keeping you tethered. Denial can be the one coping mechanism getting you through the day. To be clear, it's not like I'd look in the mirror and see someone thin. It was more about *not* looking in the mirror in the first place. Or believing that my weight was something fleeting, like a pimple. Maybe when I woke up the next day, I'd be thin, the sheets wet with the fat that had magically melted off during the night. I refused to let the magnitude of my weight sink in because if I did, I'd have to face reality. And, at thirteen, reality was no friend of mine.

I had other troubles. Around that time, I developed gynecomastia, a condition in males where your estrogen and testosterone levels get all fucked up. Basically, you grow breasts. In my case, it wasn't so much breasts that were the problem (I was already top-heavy in that department, as you can imagine) as it was my nipples. They puffed out. They went from looking like wrinkled raisins to the cherry-red tips of badminton birdies. And they were very noticeable. Naturally, I was horrified. It was the absolute last thing an overweight burgeoning homosexual needed. My rebellious nipples were yet one more secret I had to hide.

I went to the doctor, who was pretty useless. Give it time, he said, my hormones would settle down. But I needed an immediate solution. I had to go to school the next day. And the day after that. Warmer weather was on its way, and it would only be a matter of time before I had to trade my jackets and sweatshirts for lighter, less forgiving clothing. So I came up with a solution on my own.

I taped my nipples every day. At first I used Scotch tape, but that didn't hold very well against my skin, especially when I perspired beneath my clothes. So I moved on to wrapping masking tape around my torso. It was awkward to do, and the binding around my chest meant I had to be careful not to take any deep breaths, but, for the most part, it kept my secret safe.

Isn't adolescence a batshit time? I mean, there I was, an overweight thirteen-year-old, wrapping masking tape around my body every morning, and never once did I stop to say, "What am I doing? This is nuts." There was no questioning it, because to question it would have meant an admission—of my failure as a boy. It would have meant bringing the monstrosity of me out into the open. And that was the last thing I needed. There's a strange solace to be found in the secrets we labour to keep, the rituals we perform, the pieces of ourselves we try to conceal under our clothing. So long as we're the only ones who know how screwed up we are, we feel safe. The universe will protect us, but we must be vigilant. If our secrets get out, if our true selves are revealed, we'll be rejected, reviled, humiliated. Whatever shreds of dignity we have left in our fat, taped-up bodies will be trampled into the ground.

I shouldn't complain too much. My nipple and weight issues ended up being fodder for my first book, *Fruit*. I wanted to reclaim that period of my life, to own that dysfunction for what it was, even if only through the pretense of fiction. And my protagonist had it worse: his nipples talked to him. I don't remember mine speaking. How could they, under those layers of masking tape?

So yes, there were body issues, Dwayne. I was closeted, overweight, and had puffy nipples. It was the unholiest of trinities.

The weight, at least, was one thing I could control. My uncle, who had been overweight for most of his life, had gone to a hospital dietitian and lost over one hundred pounds after trading in his Kentucky Fried Chicken for raw cabbage. He went from bringing my sisters and me bags of penny candy to packages of Trident. (Bullshit, as far as I was concerned.) He was a lifelong bachelor and I think his weight loss represented a second adolescence, another shot at life. He'd show up at our house in jeans (!) or sporting a purple faux-fur fedora. And because I had always thought of my uncle as a bit of a joke in the way that relatives sometimes seem to teenagers, it bothered me that he had reached the other shore, where all the thin, happy people resided, whereas I was still stuck where I had always been, Jack Horner with my thumb—and every other finger—in the pie.

My oldest sister, who was also overweight, was the first to follow in my uncle's footsteps. Soon after she went to the same dietitian, the dynamic in our household shifted. Our fridge was stocked with cans of Tab, the freezer loaded with boxes of Lean Cuisine four-cheese cannelloni and sweet-and-sour chicken, the cupboards full of Sugar Twin and packages of Crystal Lite iced tea mix. Now there was another traitor in our midst. While being overweight can be a lonely experience, there's solidarity in being around your fellow fatties. So long as you're all overweight, none of you are overweight.

Don't ask me to explain this psychology.

It wasn't long before I wanted a piece of the (calorie-reduced) pie. So I went to the hospital dietitian, too. I remember sitting next to my dad in the waiting room, eyeing the other overweight people, comparing myself, taking inventory of everyone else's body, how my fat compared with theirs.

"Two hundred and three pounds."

That was what the dietitian announced when I stepped on the scale. Her voice was so matter-of-fact. This was a woman who spent most of her days weighing fat people, after all. I'm sure I wasn't the largest thirteen-year-old she'd ever weighed. Or was I? A part of me waited for her to pick up the telephone. "Hello, Guinness Book of World Records? You're not going to believe this but . . ."

I was ashamed, naturally. I hadn't stepped on our own bathroom scale in years. Hearing that number spoken aloud was like being thrown into a cold lake. My weight was an insurmountable obstacle, a mountain where the top wasn't even visible due to crowning clouds.

After my weigh-in, the dietitian sat me down to review my eating habits. She set out rubber replicas of food on the table between us. A grey pork chop. A hard white pile of mashed potatoes. A bumpy mound of bright green peas.

"How much would you say you eat of this, Brian?"

"I don't eat rubber peas."

She tried to be encouraging. She told me that when her husband got a sundae, all she ever needed was a spoonful. "I just need one bite and that's it," she said with a smile and a goofy shake of her curly hair. "That's all I ever need."

I immediately felt sorry for her.

I was put on a plan, outlined in a printed tri-fold brochure that I tacked onto the fridge. Everything was about portions. I'd need to weigh my food. Cut wieners in half. Drink water instead of Coke Slurpees.

It was awful in the beginning, this self-control business. But I stuck to it, because it was new and a challenge and something different for me. I wanted to be thin more than anything. Once my mind switched over, once I believed I could be good-looking, thin, and popular if I wanted it badly enough, there was no stopping me.

I would become someone else. Someone *not me*.

I lost eight pounds in my first week, which felt like a miracle. Losing weight was so easy!

But, as I'd soon find out, weight loss doesn't maintain that momentum. It only gets harder. You can go from week to week without losing anything, even if you've been very good. Well, mostly good. And that's when the frustration would set in and I'd find myself with a bag of Mr. Christie's Pirate oatmeal peanut butter cookies. I'd twist off the outside cookie layers and devour them before mashing the stacked icing discs together into a ball, which I would slowly, almost hypnotically, nibble on while I watched *Creature Feature* on a Saturday afternoon.

I fell off the diet, went back on, fell off, went back on. Anyone who has struggled with food, or any other kind of addiction (someday, Dwayne, I'll write to you about smoking), will be familiar with this. There's rarely a guiding light that keeps you moving towards a cleanly marked and defined destination.

My weight fluctuated throughout high school, though I was never as heavy as I'd been at thirteen. My gynecomastia cleared up, eventually, but it took so long. All those years of hiding my body, of never feeling confident or normal, left me fucked up about it. There were boys everywhere whose bodies looked and behaved in the way they were supposed to. I felt so betrayed, so denied, by this body of mine. But which of us had betrayed the other first?

By the time you sent me your letter, I was rail-thin. A student diet of sardine sandwiches and Matinée Extra Milds will do that. And while I had always dreamed of being thin, I also quickly learned that thin wasn't the end goal I'd always believed it to be. Now I had another issue to contend with: my lack of muscle. I was soft, Dwayne. Arms like twigs. Stretch marks like scratches. Love handles that spilled over the waistband of my jeans.

It's funny. It's not until you share your body with someone else that you realize how imperfect it is. Up until that time, I could be solitary in my insecurities. No one needed to know about my body, since I wasn't revealing it to anyone. But I had entered a new arena: the sex arena. And it's awfully hard to be erotic wearing a button-down. Lights would have to be low. Sheets pulled up. In truth, I'd never be able to really enjoy sex, or just completely let go, because I'd be too conscious of my partner's experience with my body.

"It's like you have a layer of fat over everything."

Someone I was dating once said this to me. Yes, he was an asshole. But the comment stuck. Obviously. What he said was insensitive, but it wasn't untrue. The person I'd been trying to escape, the overweight thirteen-year-old with the taped-up nipples, he was never as far behind me as I would have liked.

I've been thin for over thirty years now. But in spite of how I look, fat is still the lens through which I view the world. A part of me is still stuck at thirteen, and in many ways, he's the person I identify with more than any other version of myself from any other time in my life. Maybe that's true for all of us. The person we were when we were the most lost, the most vulnerable, the most beaten down, the most hidden, is who we want to protect. Keeping him here, in the cradle of my arms, means that he's safe. No more harm will come to him. Not on my watch.

Now I've got my fifty-year-old body to contend with. Everything is drooping. Varicose veins ripple along the back of my right leg. My knees crackle when I go up and down the stairs. I have rings of hair, like tumbleweeds, around my nipples. (Just imagine ripping masking tape off them now!) My love handles are a constant threat. I'm always readjusting shirts and sweaters, pulling down corners and edges, even when I'm by myself. I step on the scale every day and step away feeling either that I've managed to escape something or that its shadow looms on the horizon.

As I get older, I need to take care of myself. And I also need to let go. I'll never have a body that I'll be entirely comfortable with, one that will make me want to walk around naked in front of someone when the lights are on. A body that I'll forget during sex, that I'll send a photo of to a stranger as a selling point.

But here's something you might appreciate. A couple of years ago, I joined a gym for people over the age of forty. It's a relief to be among the seniors as they power-walk on the treadmills or do their stretches on the mat. I don't feel defeated before I start. I don't compare. I don't give a fuck what I look like either. I wear cheap shorts and free promotional T-shirts. I put my earbuds in, listen to nineties dance music (specifically *Club Cutz Volume 4*), and talk to no one. There's a satisfaction in knowing that I'm not simply on the sidelines.

Maybe I'll see you at the gym sometime. I'll be the one in the Ontario Society for the Prevention of Cruelty to Animals T-shirt, bench-pressing seventy pounds like a motherfucker.

Sincerely,

Brian

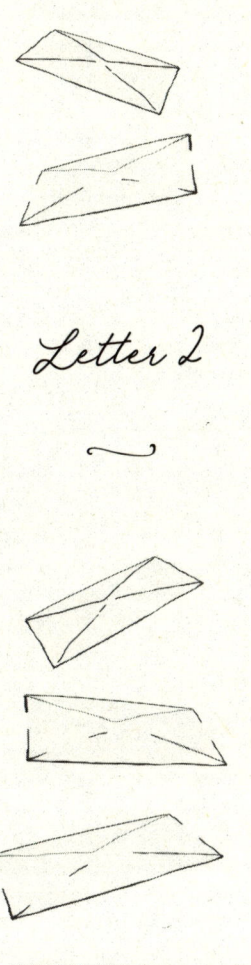

Letter 2

Dear Gorgeous Blonde Hunk!!!

I don't normally resort to answering ads like this,
but like you I'm tired of being alone. I'm 28, 5'7", and
145 pounds of solid muscle—NOT!!! I find myself unable to
meet men whom wish to pursue something of substance. Each
time I allow myself to think that "he" might be the "one"
the train goes completely off the rails and I find myself
alone, bored stiff. (Interpret that any way you wish.)

I'm going to stop here. Now it's YOUR turn. I will await
your reply. My address is included. Do NOT forget to
include a photo!!!

                                        Sincerely,
                                        Snuggles

P.S. Don't hold back. I'm open to ANY questions you have.
     You have my assurance that discretion will be used.
     (By both of us I hope???)

                                        Snuggles

Dear Snuggles,

Call me presumptuous, but I'm going to guess that you were never in the running for the title of Mr. Masculine of the Universe. I realize that reading my words might cause you to bristle even if you were reclined on a chaise longue, eating bonbons and wearing a silk robe trimmed with ostrich feathers. It always seemed like a low blow, calling out another gay man's masculinity—or lack thereof. To be called a screaming queen wasn't exactly a slur, especially if it was another queen calling you that, but it was definitely a means of putting—and keeping—a gay man in his place.

I could be wrong about you, though. Maybe you were happily in touch with your feminine side. Maybe, unlike me, you had managed to rise above that gender landfill and see all the masculine/feminine bullshit for what it was.

A trap.

And yes, even yours truly had played right into those polarities in my personal ad, casting aside the Princess Di and Rambo wannabes. At the time, I thought I was being clever, but I see now that I was sending a very transparent and exclusionary message about the types of guys I was interested in—and the types I wasn't.

Some of the respondents to my ad (including the ones I replied to) used the term "straight-acting" to describe themselves. The whole "straight" thing was considered such a selling point, wasn't it? Like saying you had a car with leather seats or that you were well-endowed. "Straight-acting" was regarded as an achievement. It meant you could pass as heterosexual and manoeuvre successfully through the world. Of course, for many gay men, masculinity, or at least the appearance of it, was a means of survival. From a young age I knew that the more feminine a male acted, the more he was a target. And it wasn't long into my coming out that I also learned that the more feminine a gay man was, the less desirable he was. Even among the gay community, feminine gay men were often desexualized, perceived as caricatures or there mainly for comedic relief, always cast in the best friend supporting role but never the romantic lead.

You don't need to look much further than gay pornography to understand the standards the gay community had internalized. The first gay porn I bought (a VHS tape, Snuggles) was called *Dick Dreams*. I won't go into detail about the intricate plot lines, but let's just say there was some questionable behaviour going on at an abandoned warehouse and Detective Dick was assigned to get to the, er, bottom of it. Dick had all the makings of a tough-talking detective: the suit, the snarl, the big gun. But as soon as he opened his mouth, the purse fell out. And while the rest of the characters didn't seem to pay too much notice (they were preoccupied with other things), Dick's effeminacy extinguished my warehouse fantasies. I thought of him as someone to mock. When I was around my gay friends, I'd often impersonate him during his various scenes. "That'sss it. Sssuck that cock, you cocksssucker!" We'd roar with laughter.

As gay men, we had been conditioned to dislike one another so much, to devalue the expression of our femininity, that we ended up turning against ourselves and upholding the pillars of the straight world—the same world that had shamed us in the first place.

It never even occurred to me that, when it came to my impersonations of Detective Dick, the joke was really on me.

I don't know about your childhood, Snuggles, but by the time I started kindergarten, I understood that the world was divided between feminine and masculine. Television commercials told me that only girls played with Easy-Bake ovens and only boys played with Tonka trucks. At school, girls lined up on one side of the hallway, boys on the other. At recess, boys could chase girls, but rarely would girls chase boys. (And boys never chased other boys, much to my chagrin.) Even my superhero bedspread and matching curtains featured only muscular men in tight costumes. (Not that I was complaining.)

And what did those messages say to a boy like me, who wanted to be chased and dreamed about making cherry chip cakes in an Easy-Bake oven of his own? A boy who was more interested in a Holly Hobbie rag doll than Evel Knievel and his Stunt Cycle?

Where did I fit in?

From my perspective, the world of girls seemed like such an easier place to reside. I'm not saying that girls had it better than boys, because they didn't. But things seemed less con-strained for girls, more fluid. They appeared to have more options. Pants or dresses. Short or long hair. Ultra girly or tomboy. When a girl strayed towards more masculine attri-butes, it didn't carry the same negative connotations it did for boys who ventured towards the feminine. And that had more to do with how femininity was viewed from the get-go. Regardless of whether you were a boy or a girl, femininity was a hallmark of weakness. Masculinity signalled strength.

When I was seven, I wanted a Barbie doll. I know, I know. It's a total cliché. So many gay men have childhood Barbie doll stories of their own. But we were living in isola-tion from one another, unaware there were other boys like us everywhere, so sharing these stories can be therapeutic. Reclaiming my Barbie doll desires makes me feel less alone, less of a freak, even all these years later.

A girl friend of mine had the full Barbie works: the car-rying case, the shoes, the tiny plastic hangers, and all the outfits. I'd go to her house on Saturday afternoons and be enthralled by her collection. Jealous, too. I didn't think it was fair we always had to play with *her* dolls. She could be bossy about what the Barbies were and weren't allowed to do. Unfortunately, this meant I was forbidden to grind Barbie's and Ken's smooth, plastic crotches together. I wanted nothing more than to level the Barbie playing field by showing up for our next play date with a stocked carrying case of my own.

One day, my mom and I were in the toy section at Woolco. I asked if she could buy me a Barbie doll. I pointed one out on the shelf, the doll's blue eyes gazing blankly from behind the plastic shield of her box. I don't even think she was a real

Barbie, but a knock-off. I must have thought I stood a better chance of getting the discount version.

"Oh, Brian," my mom said dismissively. "Don't be stupid."

"Please?" I asked, batting my eyelashes. I had recently written in a school report that I had the second-longest eyelashes in my family, so why not use them to my benefit?

"Absolutely not."

"But why?"

"Boys don't play with dolls."

I pleaded with her. I may have even managed to work up some tears. My parents had had me later in life ("We had too much Captain Morgan rum the night you were conceived," my mom would often say), and from time to time I'd use this to my advantage. Older parents were easier to wear down. I usually got what I wanted if I persisted hard enough. But my mom, for once, held fast, and pulled me over to the aisle of boy toys.

"Look, they have bags of plastic soldiers," she said encouragingly.

We ended up getting a Dracula doll that day. Although he didn't come with an assortment of shoes, it was a compromise I was forced to make. Unfortunately, he terrified me, and I had to keep him out of my bedroom at night.

That day in Woolco, I had received a very clear and concise message: my wanting a doll was preposterous, akin to asking for a leprechaun. In my mom's denial, I started to formulate an equation. It wasn't that she was refusing me the Barbie so much as she was refusing *me*. I understood then that the things I desired, the feminine toys that brought me pleasure, were wrong in the eyes of the people who loved me. My parents weren't cruel people, far from it, but their job was to protect their boy. And, to them, this meant correcting behaviour that was deemed socially wrong, abnormal, or inappropriate. It meant putting me in my place. I remember I had a beautiful violet betta fish with fins that swirled like silk. It swam in solitude in its small bowl and had to be kept apart from other betta fish or else they would attack one another. My dad told me once that the fish would only grow as big as its glass bowl allowed, and this is the best way I can describe what my seven-year-old world felt like.

When I picked up one of my friend's Barbies the following Saturday, I felt a new shame as I fitted Barbie's white pumps onto her arched feet.

Some years later, when I was maybe twelve or thirteen, old enough to know better than to ask for dolls, a young boy brought a Cabbage Patch Kids doll to church. There was a part of every Sunday service where the minister would call the young children to gather at the altar steps for a talk about the kindness of Jesus or the value of sharing or the importance of obeying adults. When he was done, the children would walk back down the aisle towards the basement where the Sunday school classes were held. It was an endearing moment, the adults in the congregation smiling at the children as they passed. I was too old for Sunday school by that time, so I stayed in the pew, and I remember the moment the young boy passed me with his doll. He was around seven, the same age I'd been when I asked my mom for a Barbie. He simply walked past, not seeming to have a second thought about the doll he was carrying in his arms, or anyone's reactions to it. It was so matter-of-fact. And then he was gone and I was left sitting there, sandwiched between my parents, to endure the rest of the service, holding only the printed church bulletin in my hand.

The memory of this boy and his doll has stuck with me, even almost forty years later. His was a reality I never knew. Sometimes, the smallest moments are the most emblematic, especially if those moments provide a self-reckoning, a mirroring of the boy you weren't allowed to be.

I wonder who we could have become, Snuggles, if boys like us had been celebrated rather than corrected. If our femininity had been encouraged at a young age. If the alternative scene in Woolco that day had been my mom insisting I get the Barbie.

"It's about time you had your own," she might have said, proudly.

What effect would that have had on me? Can you even imagine a world where we were simply allowed to *be*—free of the self-consciousness, the constant correction, the sense of being wrong? Imagine who we might have become, how vast the world would have seemed to our young eyes. Think of all the years we wouldn't have lost mired in confusion and darkness, the energy we wouldn't have wasted trying to deny who we really were.

Imagine how kind we would have been to ourselves. And to one another.

The good news, from my end, is that "straight-acting" is no longer a phrase in my purview. I'm on the other side of that bullshit now. "Straight-acting" is one of those terms I rarely think about these days, like "popular" and "cool" and "fat-free." I'm not preoccupied with whether people think I'm gay-acting or not. And who cares if they do?

I'm inspired to see the rigid binaries of masculinity and femininity being questioned by the emerging generations. And I'm grateful that the constructs of gender are loosening. The more we're able to define ourselves, rather than being defined by others, the more authentic we are and the more we'll shine. And isn't that something we all deserve? To burn brightly in an overcast world? To feel contentment on our own terms and not have to worry about the pieces of plastic we choose to play with?

To be honest, Snuggles, sometimes I feel like I'm a bit late to the conversations around masculinity and femininity, that the time I grew up in and its constrictions have been too ingrained in my perceptions of how I see myself. It isn't as easy for me to dismantle ideas of gender as it might be for someone younger. I will always feel a weight of "wrongness" on my shoulders. I'll never know what it feels like to truly be myself, unconfined, wide open.

I don't think I'll ever know how big I could have grown.

Sincerely,

Brian

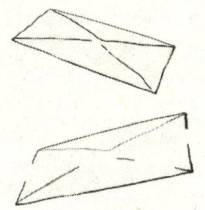

Letter 3

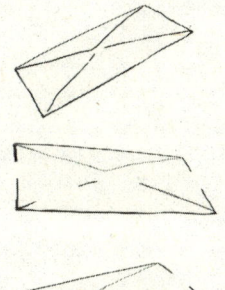

HI.

SAW YOUR AD IN THE NEWSPAPER.

NOT BAD!

I'M NOT A PRINCESS OR A SYLVESTER STALLONE
TYPE. BUT I LIKE TO THINK I CAN HOLD MY OWN.

THERE'S A GOOD CHANCE I'M OLD ENOUGH TO BE
YOUR DAD. BUT LIKE I SAID, I CAN HOLD MY OWN,
SHOULD IT BE REQUIRED.

LONELINESS CAN BE CURED WITH A
GOOD DINNER AND BOTTLE OF MERLOT.

WHAT ARE YOU WAITING FOR?
CALL ME.

REG

Dear Reg,

Do you really believe that loneliness can be taken care of that easily? I mean, it always seemed more complicated than that. To me, anyway. Especially when I was twenty-one. Loneliness was a garment I wore. I've never had anything fit me more perfectly.

But after rereading your letter, I realize how much I'd screwed up. All those years of loneliness and all I needed was a bottle of Blue Nun and a chicken cutlet? If only I had known that in 1992. How much less lonely I would have been, not to mention I could have saved myself sixty-five dollars on that stupid ad. Happiness had been within reach all along. I just needed some cutlery and a corkscrew.

Oh, I'm only horsing around with you, Reg. I don't think you meant that loneliness could *literally* be cured with wine and a good dinner. After all, you were replying to my ad, which would imply you were a bit on the lonely side yourself, if you don't mind my saying. And we've all seen what happens when you rely on food and booze to cure anything. You find yourself waking up in the gutter, the rain pelting down on you, mascara running, your belly flopping over the waistband of your too-tight jeans. It's a nice idea, though, isn't it, to think that whatever troubles us could be so easily fixed.

If only loneliness was that simple to cure.

I'm nattering. I realize that. But I'm stalling, you see. There's something I need to tell you, something important, and I'm not sure how to begin or where to start. It's a sordid tale, but I think you might be up for it. You sound like the all-ears type. So rather than continue to beat around the bush, I'll just come right out and say it.

When I was nine, I stopped shitting.

It wasn't because of cheese or a lack of fibre. I wilfully stopped myself from crapping. The urge would come over me, strong spasms racking my body like an accordion being squeezed, and I'd furiously fight back as if I were waged in a battle where I was the priest and my turd was the devil.

I don't know what triggered this phase in my life. I don't recall a traumatizing toilet episode or ever having a bad public restroom experience.

As you likely know, you can't not shit. At least, not for an extended period of time. There are repercussions when you try to stop your body from doing something it deems necessary. Every now and then, the shit would win. (Later in life I'd come to learn this lesson more succinctly.) Mistakes would happen, and I'd leave evidence of my lost battles in my underpants. I was horrified, of course. But this only intensified my need for secrecy. To let anyone find out would have meant disaster for me. So, like any logical child of that age who is crapping himself would do, I tossed the soiled underwear behind my bedroom dresser to keep my secret safe.

This went on for some time. Although I can't remember exactly for how long, it was long enough for my mother to notice my depleting underwear supply. She started to get suspicious when putting away the laundry.

"I don't know where his underwear is going."

I overheard her say this to a relative. It was the summer of 1980, and we were visiting my dad's family in Saskatchewan. My family would make the drive out there every few years. I'd complain of being bored before we'd even pulled out of our driveway, my teenaged sisters would load up on their eight-tracks and paperbacks, and the trunk would be so crammed that the back bumper would scrape against the asphalt.

In Sarnia, my only extended family was my uncle, my mom's brother. He'd come to our house every other Sunday for dinner and bring his laundry for my mom to do, along with a large rolled-up tube of tabloids and magazines for my sisters and me, including the *National Enquirer*, *Star*, *Us Weekly*, and *People*, as well as the comics section from the Saturday edition of the *Detroit Free Press*.

I don't think my uncle actually read any of the magazines he brought us. Buying them provided him with an excuse to go to the downtown variety stores he'd frequent, as well as the coffee shops, to chat it up with the girls behind the counters. He was a "confirmed bachelor," to quote my mom.

"Mother ruined him," she used to say. "No girl was ever good enough for her boy."

He never moved out from the tiny bungalow where he and my mom grew up, and since the death of my grandparents years earlier, the house had become part of my family's folklore, shrouded in mystery. No one was allowed inside. The blinds and curtains were always drawn, the windows never opened. That house, in my mind, was like a fortress, sealed off to the outside world. As a child, I was obsessed by the enigma of it. The closest I ever got to seeing its interior was when my dad would drive me over at Halloween to trick-or-treat.

"What do we have here?" my uncle would announce, quickly slipping through the front door and pulling it closed behind him. "You supposed to be some kind of pirate, Brian?"

I'd desperately try to get a glimpse over his shoulder as he came out, but he was always too fast for me. For an overweight man, he was remarkably agile. He'd toss a couple of Halloween Kisses into my pillowcase (a treat worse than getting an apple, if you asked me) and then the moment would be over. I wouldn't have another opportunity like that for at least another year.

We all knew that he was a hoarder (back then, hoarders were referred to as "collectors"), but were there other things inside that bungalow? My blossoming writer's imagination ran wild. I knew the only way we'd ever get access into that house was if my uncle either died or had to be moved out. When he was eighty-seven, the latter happened. He had a fall in the kitchen. A neighbour called my mom, who called the paramedics. My uncle would never return to live in that bungalow again.

Which, I realized, was for the best once I finally stepped inside. If you've never been inside a hoarder's house, Reg, it's an eerie experience. The house was silent, but everywhere I turned, all I saw was noise. The chaos was overwhelming. I was waist-high in a sea of baseball hats, books, magazines and newspapers, plastic grocery bags, and folded shirts still in their cellophane packaging. How had he lived like this all these years? I looked at the solitary fold-out chair positioned in front of the television and was struck by sadness. He had this entire house, and yet he'd only allowed himself a few square feet of unrestricted space. Even his bed, a tiny twin mattress, was pushed against a wall in a room filled with towers of paperback books and records.

My uncle had become trapped by his shuttered world, his secret terrain. I could only assume that to live within that chaos, day after day, meant that, at some point, he must have stopped seeing it.

He'd become a prisoner of his own creation.

There were no hoarders on my dad's side of the family. In Saskatchewan, the view was as flat and far-reaching as your eye could see. There were aunts and uncles whose houses we were allowed to go inside. And talk about cousins—more than I could shake a wheat sheaf at! First cousins and second cousins and people I was told were my relatives but it was hard for me to establish a meaningful connection to them. The notion of forming family ties was too complicated, too overwhelming. At times it seemed as though I was related to everyone in the province.

My paternal grandmother also lived there and she was the embodiment of everything you'd want a grandmother to be and look like: snow-white curls, pleated dresses and blouses with bows, terracotta-coloured stockings, and black shoes with square heels that clicked on her kitchen floor as she went to load up plates with more homemade chocolate chip cookies.

That summer of 1980, we had driven out for my cousin's wedding. It was important for me to make a good impression while we were there. My insecurities made me sometimes feel as though we easterners were being judged by the relatives. As if my dad's side was taking stock of how George had done by his move to Ontario. Sizing up his family. Our manners. Our weight. Our car. I couldn't help but be self-conscious around them. Since I only saw these people every few years or so, it was hard to sink into the rhythm of these relationships, to show up on their doorsteps and act naturally. Not that they were ever anything but kind and welcoming. But they were all familiar with one another, all part of the same flat landscape, while I had to reacquaint myself with them on every visit. And I had to be as charming as possible. I didn't want who I was, or whatever my deficiencies and oddities, to reflect poorly on my dad.

Which is why my mom's comment about my missing underwear hurt me so deeply. Why was she revealing this? Was she intentionally trying to humiliate me? And how did she even get on the topic of her child's missing underwear in the first place?

"It's a complete mystery to me," I heard her say to my cousin's husband. We were sitting in my aunt's living room, the air thick with cigarette smoke and chatter.

I wish certain moments of my life had been captured on video. I'd give anything to see my expression when I heard those words leave my mom's mouth. I'm sure I looked like Drew Barrymore in the film *Firestarter*, right before she sends a flaming fireball to blow something to smithereens.

In fairness, my mom didn't know about my dirty secret. And really, can you think of a dirtier secret? She might have thought I was nonchalantly throwing my underwear out the window, offering them up for birds to use for their nests. Or I was hiding them around the house, like Easter eggs, for people to find. I could be a prankster like that. Reach into the flour canister and suddenly it would be, "Oh, Brian!" Maybe I was mailing my underwear off to children in need. That wouldn't be much of a stretch, would it? Children can be very charitable at that age.

How could my mother know what I'd been doing, even though the awful truth was right there, under her nose?

(Okay, I'll stop with all the double-entendre stuff, Reg. You're likely already pouring your second glass of Merlot.)

But when you're nine, you don't stop to think rationally about these things. You don't consider that maybe your mom's comment wasn't malicious or that her end goal wasn't to humiliate you. It was just a mother talking shit (sorry) about her kids, as moms do. Especially after having to deal with them around the clock on a two-week family vacation.

Naturally, I screamed at my mom after this betrayal. Not in front of the relatives, of course. In spite of my rage, I had more self-command than that. I unleashed the demon later, when we were alone in the basement of my aunt's house.

"Why did you say that about my underwear?"

"What are you talking about?"

"I heard you say my underwear was missing. You're trying to embarrass me."

"Why are you so upset? Look, I'm sorry. I didn't mean anything by it."

I didn't believe her. I didn't trust my mom. Not at that time in my life. If I was a puzzle, a Rubik's Cube, then it was her job to figure me out. Not just that, but it was her right to know who I really was. As her child, I was her property. She lorded over me. But the more she pried, the more I saw the wheels turning in her head, the more I resolved to never let her in and give her that satisfaction. I was convinced that she was out to expose me. How did I know she wasn't going through my room when I was at school? How did I know what she was up to when I wasn't there to watch her, when I wasn't there to guard my private domain? She could walk into my bedroom at any time and there was nothing I could do to stop her.

These are familiar battles between parents and children. It's the secrets and intimate knowledge that each holds about the other that leads to fear and frustration and a particular kind of claustrophobia.

What made things worse during that trip to Saskatchewan was that I had an accident in my underpants at my grandmother's house. I didn't have the gall to throw something behind her dresser (I'm sure it would have been the last time we got an invitation out west if I had), but my soiled underwear was discovered one day, maybe half-hidden in a closet somewhere. I don't remember.

But what I *do* remember is my grandmother washing out the underwear. She told me not to worry, that it was fine, while I stood there, mortified that my secret was now out in the open. I don't recall speaking to my mom after this, and I don't know what this did or didn't confirm for her about the mystery of my missing underwear. But eyebrows were certainly raised. The cloud of suspicion I was already under grew heavier.

I was convinced that my soiled underwear had ruined our trip. I could only imagine the conversations taking place among my relatives once our car pulled out of the driveway. What would my grandmother think of me? Worst of all, I'd done the very thing I feared more than anything else— I'd made my dad look bad. Why couldn't I be a normal son?

The most embarrassing thing was how old I was at the time. I wasn't a toddler learning to potty train. I didn't have a bowel condition that caused me to lose control of my bodily functions. I was a nine-year-old who refused to shit. Of all the things I could do, of all the habits I could pick up, *this* was what I'd settled on?

"It was our form of rebellion," one of my sisters told me years later. "It's because Mom was always after us about our bowel movements. Did we go? Had we gone? When had we gone?"

My sister says she remembers sitting on the edge of the stairs as a child, rocking back and forth, holding in her own rebellion. When she told me this, I didn't feel quite so weird, although it didn't make me feel any better either. It didn't explain things. If it was a matter of rebelling against my mom, why not take up something that didn't cause so much cramping or lead to so many missing pairs of underwear? Why not take up swearing? Soaping windows? Gathering up dead birds and conducting burials in the backyard? The things normal kids do. Not willingly constipating yourself.

Not doubling over in agony as a way of—what? Proving that my bowel movements were none of my mom's business?

Who was really the loser here?

After we cleared out my uncle's house (which involved my sister and me, a team of professional cleaners, and a hazardous-waste crew in haz-mat suits), we moved him into a home for the aged. No doubt the transition was hard for him, especially since his hoarding would have been the result of some form of anxiety, but there was no choice. He couldn't return to the life he had known. And he was starting to show signs of dementia. The place he moved to was nice enough. He had his own room, a shared bathroom.

I had naively thought the hoarding might stop in his new surroundings, but it didn't. A friend would pick him up every week and drop him off at Walmart for a few hours, giving my uncle plenty of time to restock all that we had thrown out. It was a gradual rebuilding of his empire, one baseball hat and one bottle of family-sized Listerine at a time. But it wasn't long before we got a call from the home to say there were concerns about his safety and the safety of the staff who needed to enter his room. We did another purge and asked my uncle's friend to not take him to Walmart anymore, but that didn't stop my uncle. He'd go to the Shoppers Drug Mart down the street and load as much as he could into the basket of his walker. I understood then that his compulsion to buy things, which I always assumed was more about social interaction, was beyond his control. It was only when he was found in the middle of the street on his way back from Shoppers one night that we realized he needed to be in secured surroundings. So we moved him to a new residence, this time with a locked ward he couldn't escape.

As before, he had his own room, but it was sparse. Sterile, even. How unsettled he must have felt in the silence of that barren space. And for someone who had guarded his secret world so fiercely, now he was exposed, unable to stop anyone from waltzing right into his room, whether he wanted the company or not.

I brought him some things from his previous residence: a few baseball hats, some photos, jackets, harmonicas that I had saved from the purge of his house, knowing that he used to play them when he was young and in a band. To me, it felt like giving him a piece of his identity back, a rebuilding of that familiar landscape.

His hoarding didn't stop, though. When visiting him one time, I noticed the basket of his walker was slowly filling with various items: a clock radio, newspapers that he must have taken from the common area, along with the baseball hats and harmonicas. I contemplated the contents of that wire basket, his meagre possessions, and realized with a discomforting clarity how we were more similar than I cared to admit. My uncle and I felt safest behind our closed doors, our only company the secrets we struggled to keep hidden from the rest of the world.

You're probably wondering how my sad shit story came to an end, Reg. Which it did, obviously. I'm still alive, after all. I didn't explode. What happened was this: One day, my mom discovered the pile of soiled underwear behind my dresser. This would have been sometime after we returned from our trip out west. Maybe the incident at my grandmother's house had made her more determined to solve the puzzle of her son. She could have started her investigation the day we returned, for all I know. No doubt the discovery vindicated her. It made her conversation with the relative excusable. She had been right all along.

You can hide for a while. You can keep the waves at bay, but eventually, whatever you're trying to keep inside will find its way out. That's what I'd come to understand in my late teens and early twenties, when I tried to keep something more profound in its pleasure but far more terrifying in its implications from escaping my control.

As punishment, my mom made me wash out every single pair of that crusted underwear in the toilet. She stood over me, hands on her hips, while I scraped the underwear clean with my bare hands. I don't remember what she said to me. I'm sure she asked questions. I'm sure she didn't understand. I'm sure my actions were incomprehensible to her, something to discuss with one of her friends later, in private, when I had no way of overhearing what she would say.

My shits were under probation after that. I had to call one of my parents into the bathroom to prove that I had gone.

I don't imagine this was the highlight of their day.

This went on for a little while. Until I could be trusted. Until all my underwear was accounted for and folded in neat triangles in my dresser drawer. Until I understood that I could not stop my body from doing something if its will was stronger than mine, no matter how tightly I squeezed, no matter how monstrous it would be, or how much pain it would cause when it was finally released.

When I could no longer "hold my own," Reg.

Perhaps we can discuss this over wine. I'm partial to red.

Sincerely,

Brian

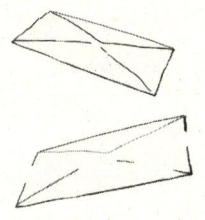

Letter 4

~

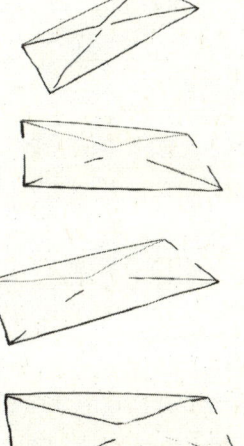

Dear "University Student"

Hi. My name is Sam. I saw your ad in the paper. I was interested so here's my reply! Well I guess I should tell you about myself. I'm 18 years old. I turn 19 on December 16. That means I'm a Sagittarius. I "hope" that's a good sign for you. So what I look like: I'm 5'9", 140 pounds, medium build, light brown hair and hazel eyes. I'm told I'm a good dresser, too. I also model part-time. In terms of my hobbies: modelling, hiking, going to the movies, music and quiet times with that special "someone."

I have two brothers and one sister and we all get along great. I like Top 40 music, mainly soft music. But not country! I'm looking for a relationship and a friendship. I was in a relationship for a year but we broke up. He was old plus an asshole. I'd like someone to spend time with, share good times with and who knows what might "happen" after that? I've included photos. They're not my best ones, but they should give you an idea on what I look like. Sorry for the messy handwriting. I'm nervous!

Well I don't know what else to say but I hope you'll write back so we can meet and get to know one another. Please write me back with a phone number and photo of you, if you can. I very much hope to hear from you.

Sam

Dear Sam,

Based on the photos you included with your letter, I think it's safe to assume your modelling career never took flight. I'm sorry if that comes across as harsh. You sounded like a nice guy. You said you had good relationships with your siblings and that you didn't like country music. All pluses as far as I'm concerned.

But those photos, Sam. The one of you on the lawn chair.

I know you were young, and far be it from me to be the asshole stomping on the supermodel dreams of an eighteen-year-old. But there's a fine line between dreams and delusions, one that comes into sharper focus the older we get. At some point, we need to confront our true selves head-on and see who we really are. It's not easy, believe me. And, in some ways, I wonder which takes more courage: to see and accept your life with all of its limitations, or to continue to stock up on dreams.

Like many queer people, I grew up confused. What made me even more confused was that I grew up in the seventies, a perplexing time for most. It was the decade of pet rocks, mood rings, rainbow toe socks, and tube tops. Nothing in my pocket of the world—in Sarnia, a blue-collar sports town of around fifty thousand back then, where there was no visible diversity and little room to be different—told me being gay was an option, that it was possible. The gay men I saw on television—not that they were ever *openly* gay—were reduced to caricatures: Campy men with quick quips who occupied squares on game shows or hosted their own fitness programs. Entertainers like Liberace and Elton John who were so completely over the top it was impossible to believe there was a real person beneath all those ruffles and rhinestones. Then there were TV sitcoms like *Three's Company*, where Jack's supposed sexuality was a running gag, signified by a limp wrist and a wink. The audience would roar with laughter, but I always felt on the edge of the joke, never quite understanding, but knowing there was something hilarious about what Mr. Roper knew about Jack. In short, I was aware there were "different" men in the world, but they were always punchlines. Inside jokes. And when they weren't there for comedic relief, when they were talking about equal rights on *Donahue* and asking to be taken seriously, they were immediately dismissed.

One spring day, when I was around ten, my dad and I were flying a kite at a nearby schoolyard. The kite was a black-and-white triangle meant to resemble a bat, but what I remember most were the kite's eyes: orange circles with red, fiery streaks. No matter how high the kite soared above me, those penetrating eyes never broke their stare from where I stood on the ground.

"I think we should have the talk," I announced to my dad. "About sex."

Wasn't I a ballsy kid? I don't know what prompted me to say this. Other students at school may have said their parents had already had the sex talk with them. Or maybe it was a joke to me. Or a dare, telling my dad what he should do. Pushing my boundaries, the way kids do around that age.

"Well," my dad said, slowly. "I s'pose."

We brought the kite down, folded it up, and walked back to the house. There was a small broom closet in the kitchen that held an assortment of items, including Sears catalogues, United Church congregation photo directories, wrapping paper, and the *Better Homes and Gardens Family Medical Guide*. It was a large book with a burgundy spine, and, in the days before you could Google the symptoms of your impending death, these sorts of authoritative books served as a catch-all, meant to diagnose and treat everything from toothaches to anal fissures. There were pastel line drawings throughout, pink-and-turquoise renderings of dissected torsos, side views of penises and scrotums, and drawings of babies being pulled from the womb by what looked to me like giant tongs. The book was a source of both humour and horror to me, and it was this book my dad grabbed before we went into my bedroom and shut the door to have our discussion about the birds and the bees.

I remember the two of us sitting on my mustard-coloured shag carpet, our backs against my bed with its superhero-themed coverlet, and the blue acrylic knit slippers my dad was wearing.

I don't recall much of what my dad said to me that day, but one sentence stood out. "There are homosexuals in the world," he said. "And they do perverted things, like lick and suck one another."

Did I know I was a homosexual at ten years old? Likely not. But I would have had some understanding of my difference, and a sense of recognition at the words my dad said. The same recognition I felt when I saw those flamboyant men on TV or when Mr. Roper rolled his eyes to the camera.

The inside joke.

I don't want to paint an unfair picture of my dad. I realize how his words make him sound today, but he was a product of his time and very few people were in support of Team Gay in those days. Truth be told, my dad was actually pretty liberal. He'd been raised during the Depression in Saskatchewan by his mother after his father abandoned the family, and I think he had a deep respect for women as a result of his upbringing. I never heard him say anything even remotely misogynistic. He was smart, too, and knew how to fix anything, a skill, sadly, I never inherited. He built the white picket fence surrounding our backyard. And it was my dad, in fact, who taught me how to use the sewing machine. He thought nothing of doing household chores like washing the floor or vacuuming. And he never put demands on me. Never told me I should be a certain way or made me feel like I wasn't living up to his ideals. He never criticized me. Not when I signed up for calligraphy class. Not when I took up the time-honoured craft of paper quilling. He never questioned the stuffed animals that lined my bedroom shelves or my penchant for baking or even my decision in Grade 8 to sign up for Home Economics instead of Shop. (I had lied to my parents and said the Shop class was full.) He never pushed me into sports. Or made remarks when my weight began to balloon. He never made me feel like I had to be something I wasn't.

And this, ironically, made me feel worse about my difference. If he had been an asshole, if he'd pushed me into sports, if he'd been critical, the anger I felt would have fuelled my queer rebellion. But that wasn't the man he was. My dad had been kind. Patient. Soft-spoken. He even looked like Mr. Dressup. The least I could do was give him the son he deserved.

But I couldn't even do that.

I did try, though. I signed up for softball. I wanted nothing more than to see him in the bleachers, cheering me on. So imagine how my dad must have felt, watching his unco-ordinated, overweight son in right field, running away from the ball he was certain was about to hit him. Or unearthing chunks of dirt and grass with every swing and miss of the golf ball. Or begging to be taken out of swimming class. (I was convinced the instructor was out to drown me. I still can't swim to this day.)

I sometimes wonder why my dad had made a point of mentioning homosexuality during our sex talk. In hindsight, it didn't seem like the kind of essential information a ten-year-old needed to know. I wonder if he suspected, even on a subconscious level, that I was gay. Or maybe it wasn't subconscious. He was an observant man and there were signs that would have given him pause, especially if he compared me with his friends' sons, as I'm sure he did.

Photos, Sam. There are always photos.

Me, at two, dancing in my sister's metallic dress. Me, a chubby fourth-grader, in a blond wig and garter, my skirt hitched high to reveal legs in pantyhose. Me, at twelve, in a black polyester (and highly flammable) witch dress, coupled with a black (and highly flammable) wig, my nails also painted black.

These photos came back to haunt me. I couldn't wait for the slide projector to click to the next image or for someone to flip the page in the photo album. Everyone laughed. A joke in a dress, that's how I was seen. A ham. But I never quite got the humour in the same way. Even though that witch's wig was terrible and I'd done a shitty job on my nails, that wig and those nails made me feel more special, more me, than any pair of corduroys ever could.

What took root inside me were the layers in the laughter. Layers and layers and layers.

I don't remember if my dad and I went back to our kite flying after our sex talk, but those orange eyes would stay with me in the days ahead, staring down from their vantage point. No matter what corner of the field I'd run to, I knew they would follow.

The day of my dad's sex talk, a door closed inside me. I had heard his words loud and clear. And while I didn't quite understand them at the time, they left their mark. I came to accept that whoever I was on the inside would never find safe harbour on the outside. And so, like many gay kids, I retreated inwards, constructing a parallel inner universe for myself, a fantasy world where I could flourish and which was more satisfying, more honest, than my reality.

At first, my fantasies were innocent enough. Scenarios where I was the best friend of the boy in my class who I just *might* have had a crush on. Or all the popular girls would fall in love with me and the other boys would be jealous and wonder what magic I possessed.

As I approached my teenage years, my fantasies began to border the edges of the forbidden, with darker, more sexual plot lines. I'd fantasize about other dads, teachers, and the husbands on my paper route. I couldn't conceptualize having sex with them, at least not at that age, but I knew that I wanted to be the object of their desire. And because I had been taught to believe that desire between men was shameful, I had free rein once I cast myself as a beautiful young woman (usually taking the form of Brooke Shields in a miniskirt and white pumps). I would imagine various setups: My car breaks down in front of the house of my most handsome paper route customer. Or I'm babysitting when the father (played by Kevin Costner) unexpectedly returns home—without his wife and reeking of whiskey. Or I'm asked by the gym teacher to stay behind at school one day. "It's time you and I got to know one another better," he'd say with a glint in his eye.

Sometimes, I'd bring those fantasies to life. When I was alone in the house, I'd rifle through my mom's closet, pick out one of her dresses, squeeze into her highest heels, and attempt some makeup. I'd prance around the house, my heels clicking on the kitchen's linoleum floor, carrying on like a sex goddess in a poly-blend dress from Sears. I'd sit in the living room and cross my legs, pretending to have conversations with men, being what I thought they wanted me to be: aloof, desirable, complicated, gorgeous.

I was paranoid I'd get caught. The back door could open suddenly. There'd be no time to change or to wipe the blue eyeshadow smeared across my lids. And how would I explain myself? I was too old to be a ham by that point, and far beyond my "cute in the metallic dress" years. I always felt sick with shame afterwards, putting my beige boy clothes back on. What if my dad had come home? Or if the neighbours had seen me? What if someone at school found out who I really was?

My fantasies were never just about sex. My yearning for approval and acceptance resided at the heart of all of them: from the jock on the football team, from my paper route customers, from the girls I wanted to like me, from the boys I wanted to be friends with, from my classmates and teachers. From my family.

If I closed my eyes and concentrated hard enough, I could almost hear my dad's cheers as I caught the fly ball.

As I got older, the feeling that there was something wrong about me intensified. My fantasies, even when they bordered on the completely ridiculous, became the refuge I needed to get me through the day. Without my air castles, I had only the darkness of my reality.

The layers of laughter.

When your fantasy world is more fulfilling than your reality, what happens, inevitably, is that it becomes the shelter you continually circle back to. My parallel universe evolved to become more intricate, more nuanced, more necessary, even after I left high school and the pressures of living in a straight world grew heavier.

When I was twenty-one and living in the house I shared with roommates, I used to dance around in my bedroom with my headphones on, pretending I was a go-go dancer.

I'd imagine all of my friends coming to watch me dance on the platform, how they'd think I was so amazing in my hot pants and football jersey, cut midriff, of course. But in real life, my friends wouldn't think I was amazing, because they were straight, and having a male friend in hot pants dancing in a cage at a nightclub wouldn't have been something to admire. I knew this, but it didn't matter. Neither did the fact that I couldn't dance very well. Or that I didn't have the body of someone who dances in a cage in a nightclub. But details, details.

I had started to lip-sync, too, mainly to female singers. I related more to the songs of women. They were allowed to tap into their emotional cores in ways that male singers couldn't.

My favourite singer was Celine Dion. In 1992, she released her English-language eponymous CD (remember CDs, Sam?), and I'd put on my headphones and play those songs over and over again, letting the heartache consume me. I wasn't pretending to be Celine—although with the right wig and a lot of chest-pounding, I could have done a decent job. In my head, I was singing the male version of Celine's voice. When I lip-synched to Celine's songs, I'd imagine myself in a nightclub filled with friends and family and anyone else whose acceptance and admiration I craved. Or maybe it was a release I sought. That could be it. Maybe I just wanted to escape my cage.

All those years later, I was still desperate for cheers. Still trying to outrun those orange eyes.

The lip-synching carried on for many years, longer than I'd care to admit. Between you and me, Sam, sometimes I still do it, though not nearly as often. I've long given up on the idea of being celebrated for a talent I don't possess. But who cares about talent? What matters is that when I need to retreat, to take refuge from reality, my fantasy world is still there, perfectly constructed and custom-made, whenever I feel the desire to return.

The odd time I do slip the headphones on, the mental set-up is different: I've withdrawn from the spotlight for many years. My fans have expressed concerns on Reddit, feverishly speculating if I'm dead or, worse, if I've become bloated. But I'm not dead. Or bloated. I'm just not hungry for fame anymore. I understand the futility of keeping yourself afloat on the opinions of others. But, on the advice of my manager and faced with the escalating panic of my fans, I decide to return to the stage for one night only. I'll show all these tight-skinned wannabes how to belt one out. I'll show them what real talent is. I'll show them what it means to be a goddamned star.

Are you still in good with your siblings, Sam? That's what's most important in the real world. But now that I think of it, there's something to be said for keeping our imagined worlds flourishing as well. There's room for both. And maybe one helps us to survive in the other.

I hope you're still walking runways, even if it's only within the perimeter of your mind.

Sincerely,

Brian

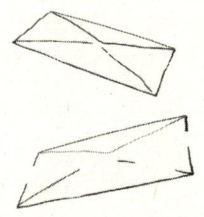

Letter 5

~

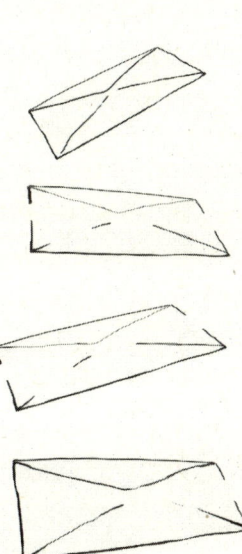

Hello Georgeous.

This is in response to your newspaper ad. I have short, brown hair and have a trim beard. I stand 6 foot 4 inches with a lean build.

I am reasonably attractive and consider myself to be an optimist. I am a teacher and I like to think this has given me a youthful outlook on things. There might be one problem though. I'm 45.

I'm interested in meeting and I hope you feel the same. I'm giving you my phone number. I have an answering machine so leave a message if I don't pick up. And not to worry. I live alone.

CRAIG

Dear Craig,

You were a teacher and you spelled "gorgeous" wrong. I hope you didn't teach English.

Maybe you were under some tight timelines while you were writing your letter to me. Or grabbing a few rushed minutes on your lunch break. Or maybe you were in between writing report cards.

I'm inclined to think you had a secret life, being a gay teacher. When I look back on my high school years, I can now zero in on the teachers I'm pretty sure were gay. Mr. Rand, the business teacher with the perm. Ms. Doucette, the butch gym teacher with the bowl cut who wore track pants and polo shirts. (I know it's a stereotype, but stereotypes usually have their origins in truth, don't they?) There were other teachers, too, although I can't one hundred percent confirm anything. I just have inklings of an undercurrent below the surface, a rippling of rainbow-coloured waves. But no teachers were out at my high school. They may have been out in their personal lives, even out within the walls of the staff room (although I'm doubtful of that), but certainly not out in their classrooms. Not in the eighties. Not in Sarnia.

What might it have meant for me to have had openly gay teachers in high school? It's an interesting question, and one that I'm not sure I'll ever know the answer to. I suppose having visible gay role models in my teenage world might have lessened the secrecy and stigma, and reassured me that being gay wasn't the catastrophe I believed it to be—even if I wasn't prepared to receive the message at that time.

I don't doubt that having an openly gay teacher would have left an impression. Many years later, I might look back on him or her with new-found respect and admiration, once I was old enough to understand what it would have meant to walk proudly down those noisy hallways, to claim your space in the staff room, to stand in front of your class, with all those eyes on you, and be unapologetically yourself.

The summer before I started Grade 9, I got a job corn detasselling. If you don't know what corn detasselling is, I don't blame you. It's the process of pulling the pollen-producing tassels from "female" corn to prevent self-pollination. And if you think that sounds glamorous, try walking through a cornfield wearing a garbage bag so the dew doesn't soak through your clothing. Or under the heat of a midday sun while the cornstalks lash your legs and arms. All this for $3.50 an hour.

But it was my first real job, outside of the paper route I'd had for four years, and I could only think of all the money I'd be making, the freedom I'd enjoy, the clothes I'd buy to start my high school career in style.

Every afternoon, a yellow school bus would pick up our teenaged crew at a high school parking lot and drop us off at a cornfield until the early evening. We truly were the

Children of the Corn. While the kids were a mixed bag, I'd venture to say that some of them were "hard living," as my mom might say. In other words, there were a few badasses on the bus. One of them was a kid a couple of years older than me who I'll call Rick. A few days after I started, Rick and I ended up walking side by side between the rows of corn. We were making small talk and he must have sensed something odd about me and decided to zero in. The conversation took a menacing turn.

Had I ever gotten laid?

Had I ever gotten a blowjob?

Had I ever eaten pussy?

The cruder the questions, the more uncomfortable I became. I didn't know how to answer him, and with each cornstalk we passed, it became clearer that I was being targeted. It wasn't long before a couple of Rick's friends joined in with the questioning. I tried my best to ignore them, realizing my best option was to say nothing at all. But this only egged them on. I was trapped, alone with them in a cornfield with no adult supervisor anywhere.

Eventually we made it out of the row and I took off as quickly as I could for the far side of the field. But on the bus ride back, Rick and his friends cajoled a girl named Angie to sit on my lap and ask me sexual questions. The crowd around us roared with laughter. I managed to get her off me and went to sit at the front of the bus, amid a chorus of boos.

I felt sick with dread. What had I done to provoke these kids? What had they seen in me that I hadn't seen myself? And how could I face the prospect of being left with them in a cornfield again?

Although I wasn't often bullied, I can understand the effect it can have on kids to have to deal with this sort of teasing and torment on a daily basis. How tall and over-whelming those shadows must seem. How hopeless, if every day brings another unyielding hammer blow.

I was terrified of getting on that bus the next day, but I asked my sister's boyfriend to drop me off at the school parking lot. I thought the sight of me stepping out of his Pontiac Trans Am would give me some edge and credibility. I don't know if Rick or his friends noticed, but they left me alone on the bus ride to the fields. Maybe they had changed their minds about me, I reasoned. I almost believed I'd man-aged to escape their wrath. But at the end of the day, Rick cornered me and told me I was dead if I didn't go on a date with Angie.

I had escaped nothing.

The threat of being alone with those kids was too much, and I quit the next day. I told no one, not my parents or my friends, about what I'd experienced. I was too ashamed. If I called attention to it, I'd be calling attention to myself, inviting speculations about why I'd been targeted. I spent the rest of that summer afraid to go anywhere, convinced I'd see Rick or Angie wherever I went.

By the time the end of August rolled around, I started to feel less anxious. And there was high school to look forward to—a new beginning, with new friends who didn't know me or anything about what had happened that summer. During Frosh Week, an assembly was held in the gymnasium for the Grade 9s. I was seated in the crowded bleachers when I heard a male voice behind me.

"It's that queer from corn detasselling."

I froze but pretended I hadn't heard him. This was followed by a punch to my back. I turned around and saw it wasn't Rick but two other guys from the bus. My worst fears had come true. The cornfield had followed me. I turned back around, ignoring them, terrified of what they'd do next, but equally terrified that other students had noticed. That was all it took to become a target, for one other kid to see that I was worthy of getting punched.

A second punch hit my back, followed by a third. I turned around again and, in my toughest and deepest voice, told them both to fuck off.

That brought the situation to an end, but not the constant threat I felt from that day onwards. Every time I turned a hallway corner, I held my breath, afraid I'd run into them. They had no doubt told Rick what school I went to. Maybe one day I'd walk out the main doors to find him waiting for me. It was only a matter of time.

All I wanted was to disappear from my own life.

I haven't told many people this, Craig, but I'll tell you. I never ate in my high school cafeteria until Grade 13. The reason I didn't was that I didn't have any male friends to sit with and I was afraid that sitting at a table full of girls would draw the wrong kind of attention to myself. I had become an expert at that—understanding the difference between good attention and bad attention. In many ways, my entire life had been spent learning to navigate that distinction. On the one hand, I longed for the validation of my peers—someone simply to say, "I like you, Brian. You're cool." But I couldn't ever be guaranteed of that because I also understood there was a side of me that I wasn't in control of. It would be easy for me to slip up and to have people notice something peculiar about the way I acted. And once they grabbed on to that, once they had made up their minds about me, there would be no escape.

To be honest, I've never really dwelled that much on the cafeteria thing. It's just (another) weird piece of my life, but now that I stop to consider it, that's a lot of lunch hours. In fact, if my math is right, between Grades 9 and 12, it amounts to about eight hundred lunch hours. I don't remember what I did for all that time. In the early days of high school, I walked home for lunch, which felt like a further failure. Nothing screams "loser" more than eating a bowl of Alpha-Getti while sitting with your mom, both of you aware that at that same moment other students are sitting with their friends in the cafeteria, eating their pre-packed lunches.

I remember walking back to school one lunch hour and picking up an acorn along the way. I wrapped an elastic band around it and told myself it was my good luck charm. So long as I had it on me, no harm, no bad attention, would come my way.

An acorn and an elastic band. People usually get far more elaborate with their good luck charms. And it makes no sense: Why an acorn? Why an elastic band? But it wasn't the items themselves that mattered, Craig. It was the *need* for them. I was so desperate for protection, I believed an acorn would save me.

Eventually I started to worry that if word got out that I was going home for lunch, it would only fan the flames I felt nipping at my heels. I decided it was better to hide, to tuck myself away somewhere. I'd walk to the nearby convenience store. Or find a quiet spot in the library. Sometimes, I'd sit on the floor at my locker with others, but not if there were too many girls around. There was a church across the street from the school, and when the weather cooperated, I'd often sit behind it and eat my lunch there. Sometimes, I'd be with one of my girl friends. Most often, I'd be by myself.

A couple of summers ago, a friend from high school and I were talking about our teenage years and I offhandedly told her about how I never ate in the cafeteria. I realized, as soon as I said it, that I'd never told anyone that before. I remember the words leaving my mouth and instantly wanting to swallow them back down into my chest, where they had been for all those years. What made it worse was the expression on my friend's face. It started as shock, then concern, then melted into sadness.

"I didn't know you had gone through that," she said quietly.

It was one of those moments that almost made me cry. And I say "almost" because I'm not someone who gets emotional over things like that. I don't deny those events happened, but I somehow manage to bury the feelings associated with them. Or I separate myself from the feeling. Or I believe, in part, that the way others treated me was my fault. Maybe I had brought on those punches in the gymnasium.

I never want to be someone people feel sorry for. There were plenty of students who had it worse. And I never saw myself as someone to pity. I saw myself as someone to admire. I was a survivor. I knew how to protect myself from my peers, from their opinions and their judgements. I knew what I needed to do to make it through my teenage day and not cross any boundaries.

Not that those boundaries were easy to discern. Time and time again, I'd slip and let my guard down. And time and time again, I'd be reminded of my difference.

When I was in Grade 10, I participated in a program called Encounters with Canada at the Terry Fox Canadian Youth Centre in Ottawa. It was designed for teenagers from around the country to gather and spend a week together, doing activities and then sobbing at the end of the seven days because how were you ever going to live without these people?

There was a dance on our last night. I had taken one of my white T-shirts and pinned it to a wall, asking people to sign it so I'd have a wearable memory of all the friends I had made. By the end of the night, it was covered in signatures and comments, but there was one comment that overpowered the others.

I think you are a bit feminine.

Someone had written that in large letters. I was horrified. I had been called out. Not only that, the T-shirt had been on display for everyone to see. And now that T-shirt, which was to have been a souvenir of a meaningful time in my life, was ruined. I couldn't even bear to look at it. I didn't throw the T-shirt away—there were still kind messages written on it—but I buried it at the bottom of my closet. Every time I thought about it, all I could focus on were those burning words, as though they'd been written in neon marker.

From that moment on, I was on high alert. I watched how I sat in class (feet flat on the floor, legs never crossed or pressed too closely together—the trick was to imagine my balls were the size of grapefruits), how I talked (never overly enunciate anything, mumbling was preferred, and be sure there was no rising lilt at the end of my sentences), what I wore (pink, yellow, and any pastel colours were out of the question, as was any clothing that was considered too fashionable), and, most important, where I looked (under no circumstances ever get caught staring at other boys). I was even mindful of how I carried my binders (always at my side, never pressed against my chest). I concealed the music I listened to (Madonna and George Michael instead of the more acceptable Guns N' Roses and U2) and downplayed the things that brought me secret joy (baking, and singing and dancing in my basement to Jermaine Stewart's "We Don't Have to Take Our Clothes Off"—the theme song for closeted gay boys in the eighties). I tried to become the version of myself that I imagined everyone expected—someone who conformed to the laws within those hallway corridors. It was so hard. The daily pressure I put on myself was relentless. But I became so adept at it that by the time I graduated from high school, I was no longer the person with an acorn in his pocket. I convinced myself that I had managed to bury whatever those cornfield bullies had sniffed out—or at least suppressed it enough that I was no longer a target, which was still my greatest fear.

Would you believe that I was crowned prom king? Although, if I'm going to be completely honest, the real winner wasn't around when they announced his name, so as the runner-up, I was crowned instead. But I wasn't embarrassed at all. There was no shame in being the runner-up prom king. Just imagine what that moment felt like for someone who had hidden behind a church during lunch, for the boy who had only wanted people to autograph his T-shirt. And there he was, a few short years later, posing for photographs with the prom queen, in his Le Château double-breasted suit.

I'd count that as success, wouldn't you, Craig? The survivors always come out on top. No need to pity someone like me.

The problem, of course, was that the success carried too much weight. Every ounce of my self-worth was determined by the checkmarks next to my name on the ballot. And the success wasn't authentic. It wasn't the real me who was crowned that night. If it *had* been the real me, if I'd been out in high school, my name wouldn't have made the ballot. I likely wouldn't have even gone to the prom.

And that's what stayed with me afterwards—not in that moment, not when I was having my dance with the prom queen or when people were congratulating me, but later, when I was alone, when I had time to let it sink in. I wanted to continue to live in that bubble of acceptance, surrounded by the cheers of my fellow students, but I couldn't. Because the prom king wasn't me. He was someone I'd created to make everyone like him. Someone who had learned to play by everyone else's rules in order to stay safe.

—

After my second year of university, I moved back to Sarnia for the summer. I was returning to my student job at the pipeline where my dad worked. I had started the process of coming out by then, slowly emerging from my place of hiding. Returning to live at home brought into focus how much of my teenage years had been wasted on trying to deny who I really was. The doubt, the guilt, the insecurity—it was all for nothing. I had been chasing after an acceptance that I never needed. I was angry, and bitter about the bullshit I'd been fed and had eaten so willingly.

One May day, I went back to my old high school to see the guidance counsellor I'd known there. During this visit, I told her that I was gay and that I was sure there were other kids like me, currently walking these halls, who were in the same dark place I had been when I was in high school. I asked her what supports there were for these students, and even for young gay adults like myself. Were there any groups? Was there anyone I could connect with? She was empathetic, but said there were no resources she was aware of, other than a contact she had at Public Health and a couple of gay friends she herself had. She offered me their phone numbers.

I left her office feeling the familiar weight of those cinder blocks surrounding me. Classes were still on, so there weren't many students milling about. I walked along the speckled-floor hallways with their rows of flat-fronted lockers, and past the school library, the washrooms, and the gymnasium. I had returned to this school hoping to heal my wounds, but I didn't even know where to begin.

And I wondered how many students were at that very moment living with the same relentless pressure I had placed on myself. How many were feeling completely alone and powerless? How many were avoiding the cafeteria at lunch? And how many of those students would escape these halls only to return one day, once they had come out on the other side, to try to untangle the damage that had been done to them?

Staring down those hallway memories, I rounded the corners I was once afraid to turn, my middle fingers raised in salute.

I don't know anything about you, Craig, or what grade you taught, but a part of me can't help but wonder—did you ever look upon the faces of your students and see someone like me? Did you ever see yourself reflected? And how did that make you feel? Did you reach out, or was it better to leave things alone? Maybe it wasn't your responsibility. You had your own life to live outside the classroom.

It's unfair of me to ask these questions of a stranger, I know. And as tough as I had it, you had it just as tough, if not tougher. You were the role model, after all, the one the kids looked up to. If the faculty found out, if the kids found out, if the parents found out . . .

Fear was my biggest teacher. It taught me how to hide and how to stay afloat in the unyielding tide of that adolescent sea. I knew that if I was eating my lunch behind the church, no eyes would be looking across a crowded cafeteria at me. No targets could be identified.

But I think the greatest tragedy, the one that almost brings me to tears, was that I never once questioned why I had to hide in the first place. I never questioned those eight hundred hours. I never questioned my fear.

I never asked, "What's so wrong about sitting at a table with girls?"

So, I guess that is someone to pity.

Sincerely,

Brian

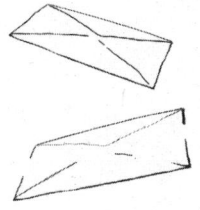

Letter 6

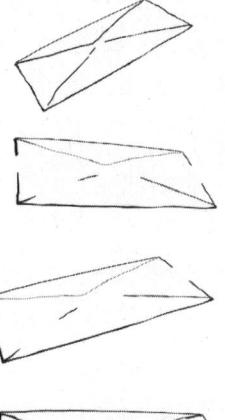

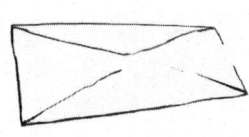

Hi.

I haven't responded to a personals ad before,
but here it goes.

I'm a 22-year-old white university student.
I'm 5 foot 8, about 135. I'm not religious
or anything and I don't have any particular
background. I might as well tell you I'm a
virgin, but there's nothing wrong with me
physically. No diseases, deformities or health
issues. I'm pretty normal, all things considered.

I enjoy sports but prefer watching to playing.
In terms of my main interest, I'd say it's my
bike. I'm not a he-man but I'm not a princess
either. I guess you could say I'm a normal "guy
next door" type. Whatever that means.

What do you think? Would we get along? It's
completely your call since I don't know anything
about you, other than what was in your ad. I'm
pretty easygoing, so hope you are too.

I'd give you my phone number but I live with straight guys and can't take that chance. Suicide isn't one of my priorities.

If you want to meet me, I'll be standing inside the main doors of the university library next Monday, Oct 5. I'll be wearing black jeans and a red jacket or just a Guess T-shirt if it's hot. I'll also be wearing my black Nike baseball hat. I'll be holding my knapsack (dark blue) in my left hand. I'll be there for about 5 minutes at 7 pm. Sorry if this sounds like a spy movie or something. But that's life.

I hope to meet you. Maybe we can find a quiet spot to talk if nothing else.

Hope to see you Monday.

Dear "Unsigned,"

We never met, even though I would have been interested in meeting you. Did I go to the library that night at seven? I honestly don't remember. Maybe I did go but just missed you, leaving me to lament that we would have been perfect for one another. My mind worked like that in those days. I was a bit of a romantic. I'd collect leaves in autumn and press them into books. I wrote poetry. I had a painting of Jesus above my door. I listened to Enya. Life was a beautiful tragedy and when something happened—or didn't happen—it was very specific to me.

I don't generally feel that way now. Not that my life is meaningless or without shape. I think it's fatigue, mainly. That kind of interest in one's own life—in autumn leaves—takes more stamina than you'd think.

You were a bit heavy with the clothing details. Couldn't you have just said "a Guess T-shirt and a ball cap"? How much competition were you going to have in the span of five minutes on Monday, October 5, at 7 p.m. inside the main doors of the library? But I understand the need for specifics. These details were important to ensure no mistakes were made, no awkward encounters took place, and the wrong person wasn't approached. Your specificity, Unsigned, was meant to protect our mutual safety as gay men.

What appealed to me about your letter is that you were closeted and living with straight guys, as I was. I shared a house in a neighbourhood where there were lots of families and trees and cars parked bumper to bumper in the driveways. It was a strange fit, a student house in the midst of suburbia.

Our house was in a perpetual state of disarray. Unwashed dishes abandoned on the counter. Furniture that looked like it had been scavenged from the recesses of our parents' basements—or the town dump. I don't think we even owned a vacuum cleaner. But, as you likely know, that's student life for you. I don't want to generalize and I'm sure there are tidy university students out there, somewhere, but I think most student houses are pigsties. It's the nature of transient student life. When you're living in a space that's only borrowed, one that you'll be vacating in just a few months, there's no real sense of responsibility or ownership. Who cares if you stain the carpet? Or punch a hole in the bathroom wall? Someone else can deal with it after you leave.

There were signs that I was gay, although my roommates didn't clue in to them—not back then, in the days before *Will & Grace*. But it was true that I was the only one to wallpaper his room and paint the trim in an accent colour (teal). I slept in an antique bed that I had refinished. And my CD collection should have been a dead giveaway. Cathy Dennis. Utah Saints. Black Box megamixes. And while these aspects might have been remarked upon and I might have been teased about the wallpaper or my remix collection, none of this necessarily pointed towards the fact that I was gay. I don't believe that was an option for my roommates. I was someone to poke fun at, to joke around with, to question, but I don't think my roommates ever seriously considered that I could be gay.

I've often heard from friends I've come out to that what I believed were my telltale signs of gaiety didn't necessarily signal homosexuality in their minds. As one friend told me, "Those were all Brian things. It was just who you were."

And while that's reassuring in some ways, that I wasn't defined as "gay" so much as "Brian," it still speaks to the lack of awareness back then. I don't want to typecast, but the wallpaper should have been a dead giveaway, don't you think? But it wasn't, because the idea that gay people could be milling about, and not just on *The Sally Jessy Raphael Show*, was inconceivable. It wasn't possible that a gay person could be your child or your sibling. Or your former girlfriend. Sure, gay people were out there in the world, wherever "there" was, but they weren't part of your daily life.

It wasn't like you were sharing a toilet with one.

I met my roommates in first year, in residence. I'd been worried about moving onto an all-male floor, especially after my high school years. Other guys made me self-conscious; I never knew how to act around them or what to say. So there I was, in the midst of moving-in-day pandemonium, my parents alongside me, our arms loaded with boxes, walking into my dorm room and meeting my new roommate—a complete stranger who I'd be sharing a room with for the next eight months. Talk about awkward introductions. He was a jock, and a rugby player to boot. (And not exactly hard on the eyes, Unsigned.) One of his first priorities was to pin up a poster of a topless woman holding a beer bottle across her breasts, printed with the words "Man cannot live on beer alone."

"Sweet Jesus," I whispered. "I'm in trouble."

Surprisingly, we got along. In fact, I got along with most, if not all, of the guys on my floor. They were goofy, kind, frustrated, sweet, insecure. Human. It could have been that not getting along wasn't an option, considering our close living quarters. Or maybe it was just that we were all so excited to be away from home and able to stay up until one on a Tuesday night drinking vodka mixed with grape Kool-Aid.

I had unnecessarily doubted myself. It wasn't as hard as I thought it would be to connect with guys. Yes, I was putting on an act, a poor attempt at machismo. I remember going through my high school yearbook with my rugby player roommate, my finger coming to rest on black-and-white photos of girls who had never even given me the time of day.

"Fucked her. Dated her. This one was in love with me, but I had to call it off before she got hurt."

Lies, pathetic lies. But I was convinced those lies were necessary to dispel any suspicions. I couldn't risk the chance of my roommate—or anyone else on that floor—finding out the truth. I was certain it would only end in disaster. And this was the ultimate catch, the refrain of my life.

So long as no one knew the real me, I'd be accepted.

But all of us on that floor were putting on a show to a certain extent. That's what guys often do, especially at that age, in the name of impressing one another.

Was residence where you found your roommates too, Unsigned?

A group of us decided to rent a house together for our second year. Things were fine for the most part. There were house politics and squabbles about whose turn it was to (not) do the dishes. But we respected one another. We weren't just roommates, we were friends.

But it was suffocating at times. You would have known what it was like, how living in a house with other guys—straight guys—was a sort of vise. A pressure on your chest. I remember sitting on the ratty couch, watching TV shows, eating tater tots or drinking lukewarm beer, and listening to the comments that flew around the room. Not that anyone meant to be mean, but we were living in different times, when nothing really got questioned. And I was afraid of what the response might be if I *did* question anything. It was easier to be silent, to lie low under those words that hung heavy above my head, like grey clouds.

Maybe, like me, there were times when you were angry or frustrated at your roommates. But mostly, I was scared that some revealing clue would be discovered, or I'd slip up and say something that would raise suspicions. Chances were, it wouldn't end well. You knew this as well as I did. That's why you mentioned suicide, although I hope you weren't serious about that part. But it wouldn't have been out of the realm of possibility back then. You and me, we understood that.

Halfway through that second year, however, things began to shift. Or rather, *I* started to shift. The gay thing kept calling. One night, my roommates and I went out to celebrate some birthdays, including my own. I was turning twenty-one. I got drunk, and when my friends weren't looking, I staggered off to the gay bar that was a couple of blocks away. I had been to the bar the year before with a lesbian friend while pretending to be "straight" and "cool with it." There was no sign or marking indicating the door that led up to the bar, so god knows how many doors I drunkenly tried to open before landing on the right one. I met some people that night, hooked up with the DJ (it's a rite of passage), and officially launched my coming out to the backdrop of "Finally" by CeCe Peniston. This was the start of what I'll call the Great Gay Divide. A corner had been turned and there was no going back. I didn't want to go out to straight bars or feign interest in girls anymore. I was tired of pretending, exhausted by the show I had been putting on for my roommates for the past two years—and really, for my entire life.

Within weeks, I swapped out my straight friends for a new circle of gay friends. And I wasn't as much a part of the house, of its dynamic, as I had been. That's what it felt like to me. My roommates didn't seem to notice or care, and yet my nerves made me hypersensitive to any little comment they made. But whatever I felt was owed to me, whatever lost time I was making up for, whatever my fears, the bottom line was that I was lying to my friends. Lying about where I was going and who I was seeing. I told myself that it was the price of maintaining my two worlds. But eventually, the barricades I'd created to keep those worlds from colliding began to crumble. Guys would call the house, voices and names my roommates didn't recognize, and I'd get defensive when questioned. Someone left a huge Valentine's Day card on my doorstep once. (Luckily he wasn't seen by anyone, but can you even imagine how I'd dig myself out of that one, Unsigned?) I'd stay out all night and be vague about my whereabouts when I came home in the morning. Again, these weren't just my roommates, they were my friends. So why was I being so strange lately? If I was seeing a girl, why was that something to hide? Why the secrecy, Francis?

I was the one who suggested that I move out for our fourth year. I needed my own space and I was officially dating someone. I didn't want to have to keep sneaking around with my boyfriend or risk the chance of being overheard on the phone with him. I didn't want to have to keep up the lies. I wanted to finally feel free. To date. To have sex in my own bed. To fall in love. I needed to get away from my friends so that I could finally deal with the person I'd been avoiding for all those years—myself.

I felt guilty about causing this upheaval and inconvenience for my friends. And there wasn't a good reason for it, or at least not one I could honestly tell them. I don't know if they were angry or if they had known this was coming. "Francis hasn't been part of this house for months," they might have said to one another.

But in spite of everything, I wanted to maintain our friendships, to try to fix the bonds that I had broken and explain the reason for my absence, both physical and mental.

So I made the decision to come out to them. Now that we'd be living apart, it would give them time to get used to the idea that I was gay. My gay friends told me not to bother. It wasn't worth it, they said. What was the point, we were all going our separate ways anyway? But that *was* the point, I reasoned. I didn't want us to continue to drift apart. I needed to take responsibility for these friendships, and to honour our shared history with one another.

I sat down to write them a letter, but my nerves got the better of me. So I waited until we were done our school year. Until our final exams were written and the furniture had been cleared out of the house and we had all returned to summer jobs in our hometowns. A few weeks after that, I sent this letter to them.

MAY 26, 1993

Hi guys.

I had originally planned to give you this letter before we all moved out, but with exams and all, I couldn't find the time. Besides, the circumstances had to be right. To be truthful, I've been postponing this letter. And I don't really want to write it, but I feel that I have to. And I have to get this out to you before too much time passes. Right now, you're probably wondering what the hell I'm talking about. You're gonna have to be patient with me, because this is really scary and I can't say that I'm looking forward to telling you what it is that I want to say. But I can't walk away from our three years together without saying something. As I said, be patient with me.

Before I start, let me just say that in all honesty, I had a really great three years with you guys. I don't think I could have asked for better roommates or better friends. And, as a general rule, good friends should always be honest with each other, right? Even though that may mean the end of a friendship. This is what I'm most afraid of. Nevertheless . . .

As you've probably noticed, I've been a little different the past two years. I've become more distant, going off to different places, meeting up with different friends. And I have to hand it to you guys. If I had been you, I would have been pretty pissed off. Suddenly, I'm not there and our friendship suffers as a result. I apologize for this. I never wanted our friendship to drift, but there were a lot of things going on in my life which inevitably caused me to drift away from a lot of people that I was once close to.

I've been telling a lot of lies the past three years and for this I'm really sorry. But I felt that I didn't have a choice. You see, guys, I'm gay. I'm not kidding. I wouldn't joke about something like this. I can imagine that this is probably coming as a big shock right now. Please continue reading this so that I can have a chance to explain myself. Maybe then, some good will come out of this.

I've always known I was gay. Some people have a day of "revelation," but for me, I've always known. Even before I knew what the technical term was.

Being gay wasn't something that I accepted easily. This year was pretty rough for me because I was living a double life. On the one hand, I valued your friendship, and on the other, I was scared that if you knew about me, our friendship would be over. I wanted to keep things in the house as calm as possible, because school work suffers as a result, too.

I'm sitting here racking my brain, trying to think of all the questions you would ask, trying to get all of this down in a coherent manner, but I'm not so sure I'm doing a good job.

A lot of my friends said I was stupid for writing this letter. They said I should walk away. But I couldn't do that. I had to be truthful. Friends deserve to know the truth, no matter how painful it is to tell it.

Please give yourselves time to get used to this. It's taken me twenty-two years to become comfortable (somewhat) with it. I don't expect you guys to be OK with it any sooner. If this is, in fact, the end of our friendship, I can't say that I will understand, but I will reluctantly accept it. What other choice do I have? If you can't accept this, then at least I'll know that straight men and gay men can be friends, can be roommates, and more importantly, can relate to one another. The past three years have proved that to me.

Sincerely,
Brian

Reading this letter all these years later makes me cringe. So. Much. Drama. But coming out *was* dramatic. I didn't know if I was going to lose their friendship, if those memories of our time together would forever be tarnished. I could be ostracized, only this time it would be for the person I truly was, not the person I was pretending to be.

I consider this letter to be one of the milestones of my life. Writing it was one of the bravest things I've ever done.

It was specific to me. And I had no idea what would happen.

There are moments in every queer person's life when it's tempting to simply turn your back on the truth of who you are. When choosing silence over honesty feels like the easier path. And there's the emotional weight to consider. Coming out, no matter what the response to it, will have an immediate effect on your emotions and your mental state. It's both empowering and terrifying. It gives you armour and yet exposes you. Everything is about to change, to shift. There's no predicting how someone will react. Everything hangs in the balance, while you hold your breath and wait for those first few words of response.

But without that risk, where's the gain? Without placing your trust in other people, how will you ever know they won't let you down?

My roommates didn't let me down. They didn't turn away. They immediately reached out to me. But I also knew there was a long road ahead of us. That's one thing I've learned. There's the initial reaction that someone might have when you come out to them—

I didn't know.

I'm flattered that you trusted me enough to tell me.

It must be so hard for you.

—and then there's the reaction that comes a few weeks or months later, once they've had time to mull things over.

So you were lying to me that entire time?

Are you sure something in your past didn't cause this?

I walked around in my underwear in front of you.

There were issues we had to work through. The lies, my secret life, the perceptions of "otherness." They had to reassess who I was and come to terms with the idea that one of their friends was gay. They had to question their own prejudices, those living room comments.

But I've also come to learn that, eventually, if you hang in there, if you're patient, if you count to ten as many times as you need to, you can usually make it through to the other side. My former roommates and I continued to hang out in our final year. We went drinking and acted just as stupid as we did before. We have been good friends ever since.

Decades later, and less than a year before he died of a heart attack, one of my old roommates came across my coming-out letter again and texted me.

"I read it again," he wrote, "and I can only imagine how difficult it must have been to write it. As your friend, I want you to know that your sexual orientation didn't mean anything to me, now or then. You are Brian, my weird friend from Sarnia. I'm sorry that you had to live life afraid to express who you really are inside."

Imagine what it felt like to read his words, even all these years later. This was how our story turned out, even if it was impossible for me to believe at a time in my life when there were only clouds.

I'm sorry I didn't meet you that day, Unsigned, for whatever reason. I hope the five minutes that you waited weren't too stressful. I hope you didn't run into one of your roommates. I hope no one asked who you were waiting for. I hope you made it out of the house okay. I hope you're happy.

Sincerely,

Brian

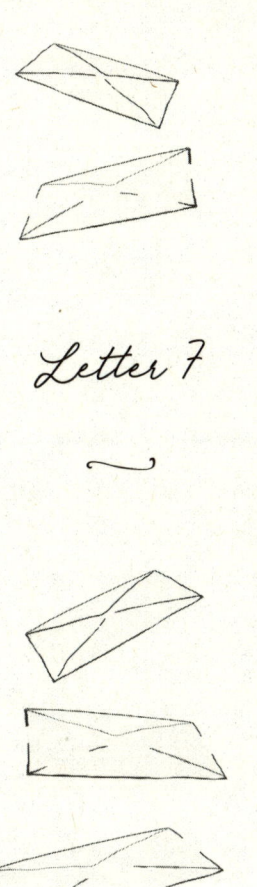

Letter 7

Hey!

Your ad was great. I bet you're a cool guy to hang out with. No point beating around the bush. I'm already 28. Is that too old for you? Hoping not. I bet we could have some fun times together.

I majored in French and Geography. I'm interested in art, landscape photography and wine. I like to work out and wrestle. I'm 5'10" and 170 lbs with short black hair.

How about you?

In my mind, you're 6 feet with dark hair that's just long enough to hang in front of your eyes. You're wearing a Penguins sweater with a white turtleneck underneath. You're also wearing a pair of jeans that are worn in the ass and so tight I can just make out your package inside,

nice and snug. You pull up in a Honda
Nighthawk 750.

Does that look like you?

I'm wearing jeans too, tight enough to show
off my hard-on. I'm wearing a black turtleneck
underneath a New York Islanders sweater. We're
wrestling. You get me in a front headlock but
I wiggle free and take control. My hand brushes
against your cock, straining to be set free.
I help you stand up and slap you on your tight
ass. Afterwards, I pull down your jeans and suck
your throbbing cock until a massive load of cum
spurts out.

Does this sound like you?

I'd like to meet you on Tuesday, October 6, at
the Wendy's at Horton and Baxter Road at 4:30 p.m.

Yours,

Patrick

Dear Patrick,

This does not sound like me. I would never wear a white turtleneck under a sweater.

Sincerely,

Brian

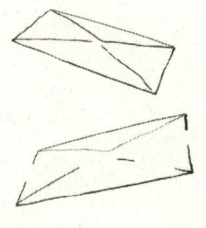

Letter 8

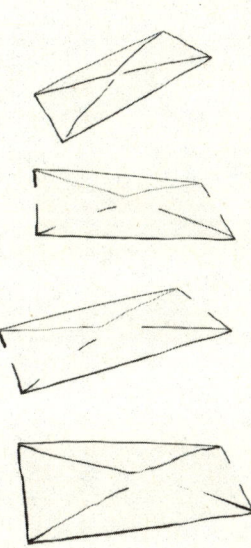

Hi! I love your ad. You sound interesting.

A little about myself. I'm 19 and in college. I'm 5'6"
with reddish-blond hair. I'm often told that I have a
boyish face and that I'm "adorable" on account of my
green eyes. I'm also straight-acting. (No one knows.)
I'm always busy on account of school. I also work part
time at the mall but I'm not going to tell you where.
Anyway, I hope this letter interests you and that you'll
write me back. I live with very nosy roommates so
I'm giving you my friend's address to write back to.

Looking forward to hearing from you.

Brett

Dear Brett,

You gave me your friend's address because your roommates were nosy? Nosy enough to open your mail? You do know that's a criminal offence, right? If so, I hope you found other roommates.

Call me paranoid, but I wasn't about to mail a letter to someone else's address. I'm not saying there was anything untoward about your letter or your suggestion. But the whole mail-it-to-my-friend-my-roommates-are-nosy excuse seemed . . . a bit fishy. Or maybe it was your real address but you didn't want me to know. In any case, you were playing games, Brett. Games. We had yet to meet and already I didn't trust you.

Trust was a big deal when I was twenty-one. It was a word I tossed around a lot in those days.

Can I trust you?

I'd never do anything to betray your trust.

How can I trust you if you don't even trust yourself?

My dating life was a love-song lyric. But a lot was riding on trust, especially since I was still closeted. I needed to take risks, to trust that other gay people wouldn't out me or call my house. That they wouldn't spread rumours about me behind my back. That someone I was dating wouldn't fool around on me, or, if he did, that he would practise safe sex.

Trust, in short, was an enormous word. It meant everything. And, as these things tend to go, trust also meant nothing.

It had its place when I was feeling pious or self-righteous. It was a way of demonstrating my worth and moral fabric. But my trust could also be bestowed on anyone, whether they had earned it or not, if the timing was right. Or if I'd had enough beer. Or, let's face it, if he was hot enough. There were so many nights when I literally put my life into the hands of strangers. I trusted them with my safety. And, honestly, wasn't that kind of trust more important than all that love-song bullshit?

It's true that if you went out regularly to the city's gay bars, you became familiar with most people who frequented them. It was a small enough community, and connections could usually be made. Someone was a friend of a friend. Or I knew someone who had dated the person. Or small talk had been exchanged at a party once. It was rare to come across a complete stranger at the bar, a person with no ties to anyone. So I usually had some assessment of character, even if those assessments were often assumptions or hearsay. There was a lot of bar-scene gossiping. Who was needy. Who was crazy. Who had a big dick, who had a small one. Which couples were into threesomes. If someone was boring in bed. Naturally, this led me to feel very authoritative about people. I was convinced I had the ability to size someone up immediately, as any twenty-one-year-old can. It's a magical skill at that age.

But what could I really know about someone?

The bar was, after all, a gathering place for people living double lives—people who had been damaged or hurt or betrayed. Growing up gay in the times and places we did had fucked us up to one degree or another. Not to say we were all sobbing heaps at the end of the night, but it was impossible to have gone through what most of us had—and, in fact, were still going through—and not be profoundly affected by it. Years of conditioning had resulted in pain, rejection, fear, guilt, low self-esteem, and loneliness. And while it would be nice to say that the bar was the only place where we were free and could truly be ourselves, I don't think that was true. I'm not sure many of us even knew how to be ourselves. How could we when we had never been given that permission? Where would we even start?

There were other places besides the bar for gay men to meet one another. Classified ads, for one. But I think we've already established that. Telephone chat lines were just starting around that time, but I had reservations about them. I was concerned that friends would recognize my voice and I'd be called out.

"Was that you on the line last night claiming to be a bi-curious jock? Girl, please."

Based on all the silent pre-recorded caller "greetings" I had to skip through whenever I called the chat line, most guys felt the same way. And what was the point of a chat line if everyone was afraid to talk?

There was also a bathhouse in the city that I went to once with a friend. I was inside for all of five minutes and kept my clothes on the entire time, paranoid I was going to be spotted by someone I knew and then get labelled a "bathhouse queen." There were a couple of public washrooms around the city rumoured to be sex havens, but I never saw anything that raised an eyebrow.

And then, of course, there were the parks.

This might not come as a surprise, but I was never good at cruising. I lacked the bravado it took to stroll through a park at night, sending out signals for sex. (And what, exactly, were those signals? A wave? Two tugs on your right earlobe? A few steps of the Electric Slide?) I also wasn't good at cruising because I needed to talk. To tell people that I was living with straight guys, that I was studying English at the university, and that I could eat a whole bag of Cool Ranch Doritos in one sitting if I wasn't careful. The talk, of course, was a mask for my insecurities. Words had always been a smokescreen for me, a means of circumvention. Cruising meant no words. No introductions. No small talk. But why would I want to deny someone my effervescent personality? Wasn't that part of the foreplay?

The truth was, I had difficulty engaging in anonymous sex. I couldn't be casual about it. I needed to date, to process the situation, to understand what the other person wanted out of life and should I consider us in a relationship now that we'd gone out for coffee twice? For me, dating was the pilot episode for the long-term relationship series. Why date if it wasn't going to go anywhere? Why spend all that energy reading between the lines, looking for red flags? Wondering if he was *really* over his ex and open to falling in love again, and if I could trust him with the most precious gift of all—my scarred and fragile heart?

I know, Brett. I'm rolling my own eyes. But that's what I was like.

I was judgy about the cruising thing, too. It seemed old school to me. Why walk through a park at night when bars were more comfortable stomping grounds? Why go to the bathhouse and wear a towel when the right shoes on a Saturday night could make you the envy of everyone? And why would anyone want to have sex in a public washroom? Sure, the threat of getting caught might add to the thrill. But the germs alone.

Don't get me wrong. The *idea* of cruising excited me. The promise of instant gratification and the escape. The riskiness. The danger. I understood its appeal. Something that had been denied to me for so long was suddenly there, in abundance, available for the taking. All I had to do was reach out.

And at times I did reach out. I parked once in a parking lot rumoured to be a cruising spot. Someone opened my passenger door and got inside. I recognized him from the bar and didn't find him attractive. He kept laughing nervously. It was so awkward. How do you tell someone to get out of your car? (That was another reason I wasn't a good cruiser—I was too polite and overly concerned about hurting someone's feelings.) I eventually told him I had exams to study for, which could have led him to logically ask why, then, was I sitting in my car in a parking lot at midnight? But he just laughed and got out. I drove off, vowing never to do something like that again.

I had also walked home from the bar in the wee hours of a Sunday morning, drunk and purposely putting myself in a situation for something to happen. Nothing ever did. Even when I went out of my way to find sex, it usually went wrong. Some of my friends picked up sex like burrs. But I never had the knack for it.

Whether I was placing a personal ad or trying to get a laughing stranger out of my car, I rarely stopped to consider my personal safety. I never contemplated the risk of meeting complete strangers. Of going back to the home—and bedroom—of someone I had just met. Of walking through a park late at night without so much as a bread knife to protect myself. Not that the city where I lived was particularly violent. But there's an undertow to every city, regardless of its size, especially at night. And who knows who I might have run into, gay or otherwise? I wouldn't have been able to defend myself.

Like many young people, I didn't think something bad could actually happen to me. Or, if it did, I assumed I'd find a way out. I was smart, after all.

I knew how to handle myself.

"The bar is no place to meet anyone," a friend once told me.

By the time I decided to place my personal ad, I had come to the same conclusion. I'd been going to the bar for about eight months by then, and I had bounced around an assortment of social circles, trying to find a group of people I fit in with. I'd hook up with one person, they'd introduce me to their circle of friends, and I'd hang out with them until the next hookup, and then I'd be introduced to a new group. At times, it felt like I wasn't dating guys so much as their friends. Yet at every turn, I failed to find the connection and community I was searching for. Coming out hadn't erased my loneliness. Imagine how disappointing it was, to spend all those years so deeply locked inside the closet, only to finally emerge and find myself still in darkness.

Sure, the bar could be fun, but it was hard to form any meaningful relationships there. How could you, when the dance music made it impossible to hear what the other person was saying? The bar could also be competitive, a beauty pageant of sorts, with people vying for attention, making snide comments, judging others.

I don't mean to paint the bar scene in an entirely negative light. Some people I met there were kind and sincere— but they didn't have a way of standing out in the crowd. And, to be honest, I wasn't really drawn to those people anyway. Not at twenty-one. I was attracted more to people who were destructive, self-centred, and dismissive of my affections. I suppose that made perfect sense, when I consider how rejection and poor self-esteem had become second nature to me. Why would those issues suddenly disappear the moment I stepped inside a gay bar? I was the same person dealing with the same issues I had when I was in the closet.

I was still struggling to accept myself.

A few months after I placed my personal ad, I started to notice a change. The romantic in me hadn't completely died, but he'd faded somewhat. I was tired of trying, of putting myself out there and never finding anyone. My failed attempts at love, the chatter of the people around me, the empty feeling of being in a crowded bar after I had exhausted every option—all of this fostered a kind of reckless cynicism. Things I wouldn't have dreamed of doing a few months prior were now real possibilities. My unhappiness fuelled my decisions. I wouldn't have called myself self-destructive, although I know that's a very real issue for many queer people. But it was self-deterioration. I stepped into situations that I knew I shouldn't. And this was new for me.

I stopped being careful.

There was a man who frequented the bar who I thought was attractive. He was older, but not out-of-the-question older. Someone I knew had briefly dated him and said he was strange, that he had seemed a bit off.

In what way? I asked.

Just weird, he said. He didn't get a good vibe. I was told to stay away.

And while most people would have heeded this advice, I didn't. This warning only intrigued me more. The man became a sort of challenge. I was attracted to the potential danger of him. I wanted to see if I could handle myself— which, of course, I believed I could.

I was playing games, Brett. Games.

One February night, I was at the bar and so was he. I struck up a conversation. He told me how cute I was and said that I had a great mouth. (If anyone ever comments on your mouth, warning bells should start clanging.) At the end of the night, the bar lights flickered on—always a sobering moment—illuminating the cigarette smoke that hung like fog and the determined faces of people who didn't want to go home alone. He invited me back to his place and

I accepted. I can't remember if I told anyone I was leaving with the man, but I would have likely laughed off whatever warnings I received. I would have told them not to be stupid. I could handle myself.

The man lived in a small apartment in a low-rise building. It was tidy, and dimly lit. A single lamp was on, but nothing more. I waited on his couch while he got us beers. I don't remember what we talked about, but at one point, we were reclined on either end of the sofa, our legs crisscrossed. I was wearing a pair of wool work socks. He took one off and started rubbing my foot. I didn't think this was particularly strange, but it did seem a bit odd. Seeing my pale, naked foot look so vulnerable in his hand brought the gravity of the situation into focus. I had made a mistake. I didn't want to be there anymore. I wanted to leave.

I excused myself to go to the bathroom in an effort to clear my thoughts. On the way there, I passed his bedroom. The door was half-open and I saw his bed. The top corner of the sheet had been turned down, and what might have been a welcoming sign to someone else now struck me as foreboding and sinister. I couldn't imagine getting into that bed with him. In the bathroom I tried to calm myself. It was the first time that I'd ever felt fear around a one-night stand. Actual fear. I tried to remind myself that the man hadn't done anything to cause that fear. I had seen no bodies in the bathtub. Smelled no peculiar smells. I hadn't spotted a mummified corpse in the bedroom. But I was in a stranger's apartment in the middle of the night, and no one knew where I was. And I couldn't shake the feeling that something wasn't right.

The bathroom window was too small to squeeze myself through, and I imagined pulling a Shelley Duvall in *The Shining* and getting stuck—that was one way to get your legs cut off. So I had no choice but to return to the living room, where the man was waiting. We made more small talk and then I said the only thing I could say.

"I should get going."

I can only imagine how confusing it must have been for him. I had come on so hot and strong at the bar not even an hour earlier, and now I'd suddenly gone cold. He dismissed my comment, maybe assuming I was joking, but I told him no, I really had to go. The more he prodded, the more he asked why, the more fearful I became. Then he started to get angry, which only made me more afraid. He told me I was ignorant. I told him he'd judged me too quickly. (Why on earth was I even debating with this man?)

"You're all the same," he spat at one point.

He could have pinned me. Pulled out a baseball bat from behind the couch. Spiked my beer. And then what would I have done? How were my smarts going to prevent me from getting killed?

I'm not saying this man would have done anything to hurt me. But I didn't know anything about him. And that was precisely the point. You can play all the games you want, but sometimes, the games play you.

He told me to get out. And this is the part that has stupefied me to this day: before I left, I gave him my number. I was afraid of this man and yet I gave him the opportunity to contact me again. Why? Was it politeness? An attempt to defuse the situation?

Or was it simply that I always felt compelled to apologize for being the person I was?

I hurried home as fast as I could, in the early hours of that freezing February morning, the city, my roommates, my parents back home, everyone I knew asleep and unaware.

He called the house a few hours later. I was sleeping, so one of my roommates took the call. I ended up calling him back and apologizing, saying I wasn't looking to date anyone. He never called back. I saw him out at the bar again a few weeks later.

I'd like to say this was the first and last time I got myself into a situation like that, but there would be other encounters to come, when I willingly rolled the dice and hoped for the best. And every time, after I was safely back at home, with the door locked, I would ask myself, "What is *wrong* with you?"

What was wrong with me, Brett, is I had grown up in a world that told me I was nothing, that I was worthless, a freak. I walked home alone late at night, looking not for sex but for a punishment I felt I deserved. No thumping dance track could drown out that noise inside my head. It would take me years to untangle those beliefs, even though the knot is still there today. Years to learn that I had worth. Years to learn the necessity of self-care. Years to learn that the only person I needed to trust was myself.

And years to learn that I was never, ever as smart as I thought I was.

Sincerely,

Brian

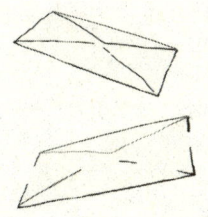

Letter 9

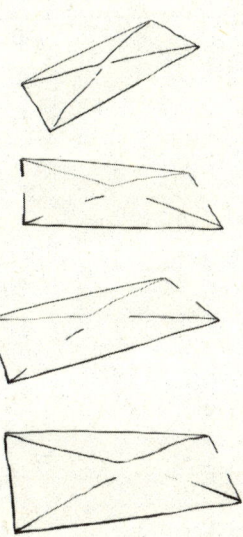

October 1 1992

To Whom It May Concern,

I am also a university student and
currently in my third year. I enjoy philosophy
and current affairs as subjects of intellect.
I am 22 years old.

My hobbies are eclectic and diverse. I
enjoy a variety of sports. I like most types
of music, travelling, meeting interesting
people and trying new exotic foods.

I am searching for someone who, like me,
is in need of companionship. It is very easy
to dwell on the negatives in life, but I have
always been someone who chooses to look at
the positive.

If this interests you, call or write me
back. It is not easy describing yourself
in a letter.

I wait to hear from you.

                    Yours sincerely,
                         Glen

Dear Glen,

Philosophy. Current affairs. New exotic foods. You certainly were the renaissance man. Especially at the ripe old age of twenty-two! The city we lived in wouldn't have been able to satiate a bon vivant like you. Not with its shopping mall food courts, its mini skyscrapers, its Mark's Work Wearhouses. The view would have been too confining, too predictable, for someone like yourself. You likely fled as soon as you graduated.

Our university town was practically buzzing with WASPs at that time, even by Southern Ontario standards. There was an abundance of old money, Ralph Lauren polo shirts (with upturned collars), Jeep Soft Tops, and a sense of entitlement as hardened as the mortar between the granite blocks of the university buildings. I don't remember much visible diversity on campus, or anywhere else in the city. Not that I would have thought to take much notice. I also never stopped to consider how homogeneous the crowd was at the gay bar on a Saturday night.

Call it a hunch, but I bet the thirteen men I'm replying to now were white. Sure, names and physical descriptions provide some indicators, but I'd put money on it. And while I didn't mention that I was white in my ad, I did say "seeks same." At the time, I'm sure I meant age. Or another student. Or gay. I know I didn't mean same as in white. That, after all, was pretty much a given.

But I do question those words and their implications now. What would a queer person of colour have thought reading my ad? Would they have felt welcome to respond? And would I have responded back to them? It's easy for me to say yes, and I honestly believe I would have, if their letter had piqued my interest. But my response would not have been instinctive.

It would have been something for me to consider.

I could be wrong about you, Glen. Maybe you decided to stay in the city after graduation, as I did. Most of my university friends either moved back to their hometowns or went to Toronto to begin their postgraduate working lives. But I wasn't interested in either option. Returning to Sarnia would have felt like taking a step backwards. And although Toronto, especially *gay* Toronto, had more clubs, more job opportunities, more men, the idea of relocating there was too intimidating for a small-city boy like myself. I was afraid I'd be swallowed up by the shadows of all those office towers, drowned out by the car horns and sirens, overwhelmed by the chaos. I'd become another anonymous face in the crowd. Given the upheaval of my university years, I wanted nothing more than to bob along in safe, comfortable waters. So I decided to stay where I was. Besides, I reasoned, I could be a writer from anywhere, couldn't I?

I had dabbled in writing throughout high school, but it wasn't until I came out that writing took on a new urgency and necessity. Up until that point, my writing had remained behind a protective wall, heavily coded and rife with subtext. Now, I was coming from a place of truth and I wanted to write about my own lived experiences as a young gay man in the mid-nineties. I dismissed the notion that those experiences were insignificant and unimportant, as I'd been led to believe for years. I told myself that my words were cumulatively filling a void.

I was aware that achieving any measure of success as a gay writer would be difficult. I knew that I couldn't simply sashay into a publisher's office, hand over my manuscript, and expect people to scramble to offer me a contract. (Although it was a nice fantasy.) I believed that I had talent. I just needed the rest of the world to believe it, too.

It was easy to get discouraged. I started stories, but rarely finished them. And the odd time I did complete a story, what then? Send it off to a slush pile at a literary magazine? Share it with friends who might not be all that interested? Most of the time, I tucked my stories—all those beginnings—in a leather folder with a brass tab on the cover engraved with my initials. At least this gave them an air of importance.

I was also struck by a feeling of pointlessness. In the real world, outside of those university classrooms where I had sat for four years, writers didn't seem to have much value. And while there was a certain prestige and romanticism in saying that I was a "writer," the hard truth was that most people I knew didn't buy books. And, of those who did, only a small fraction read the work of gay writers.

But my convictions kept me going. My anger, too. I was frustrated by having to filter my gay experiences through the lens of the straight world.

After an editor read a draft of my first novel, she told me, "I don't know who the audience for this book is."

"Me," I wanted to say. "And many others like me."

But what good was trying to convince a person that you had something of value to offer an audience when that audience wasn't even on her radar?

I knew of other gay writers who had had similar conversations with editors and agents. Who was the audience? Where was the appetite for the work? And, when a gay writer did manage to break through to commercial success, it was usually because straight characters factored heavily in the work.

"What can I say?" I remember one gay writer telling me after receiving more recognition for his latest book than he had for his previous novels. "It's my straight story."

Too often, I felt I had to chase after the permission of straight people to write stories about gay characters, because that was where all the power resided—within the realm of heterosexual gatekeepers. All I had to do was take inventory of the books I'd read during my four years as an English major to see that the literary path behind me was lined with the pages of straight narratives.

And this bias wasn't confined to the world of books. The film *Philadelphia* was released around that time, and even though it was the story of a gay lawyer with AIDS, the film was clearly made for straight audiences. Any film that casts straight actors in gay leading roles sends a signal that the film is meant for straight people. Imagine, Glen, if *Brokeback Mountain* had starred two gay men. It would never have achieved the commercial and critical success it did. Instead, it would have been labelled as a "gay" film and swept into a "special interest" category, if it had been made at all. But casting well-known straight actors in gay roles eliminates the discomfort for straight audiences. As if to say, no need to squirm in your seats—those gay characters, their emotions and their sexuality, they aren't "real." There's no threat if gay lives are seen to reside only in the land of make-believe.

I hungrily sought out gay books and films in an effort to validate my emotions and to see my own life mirrored back to me. I remember buying anthologies of gay fiction and poetry, and while it was exciting to plunge into this material, it didn't always fill the need within me. It was gay writing, but it wasn't always *good* writing. And that is what I was searching for more than anything.

Too much of the gay literature and film I had read or watched stopped at being gay. That was all they had to offer. Just another predictable story with the same paper cut-out characters, the same tropes. I wanted to write complex characters who were fully realized, complicated and messy, and who didn't conform to prescribed clichés and stereotypes. And no, I didn't need every gay lead in a film to be hot in order for me to enjoy it. Were there no stories worth telling about average-looking gay people with tummies?

To top it all off, I couldn't shake the feeling that at the tender age of twenty-three, I was already washed up. I was still jumping from crappy job to crappy job, still single, and still going out to the same gay bars, but there was no one who piqued my interest. I had no money or clear sense of direction. And after having spent almost twenty years inside classrooms, I had no idea who I was if I wasn't a student.

Video stores were a popular way to pass the time in those days, as you may recall. You could spend hours meandering through the aisles, ruminating over the VHS covers, trying to decide what sort of mood you were in, what genre would speak to you. It's not much different now, I guess, with everything online. But those video stores had very distinct personalities. Most of the ones I frequented were independents, run by film junkies who'd make recommendations even if you didn't ask. These were the days before algorithms.

There was a small video store not far from where I lived with a gay and lesbian section. One night, on a whim, I rented *Paris Is Burning*. The 1990 documentary about New York City's ball culture scene in the late 1980s follows a cast of impoverished Black and Latino queer people as they struggle to break free of their oppression. As an escape—and as a means of survival—they held "balls," which allowed them to ironically reflect the norms of the world that had cast them aside—a straight, cisgender world of wealth, celebrity, power, and white privilege. But in the ball world, the doors of opportunity remained wide open. Anything was possible with a few sequins, a good soundtrack, and an abundance of imagination. Ball "walkers" competed for trophies in a variety of categories, including "Executive Realness," "Town and Country," and "Luscious Body."

The cast of *Paris Is Burning*—Venus Xtravaganza, Dorian Corey, Pepper LaBeija, and Octavia St. Laurent, among others—were luminous and fascinating, and they dropped one-liners with seasoned street-smart wisdom. Their flamboyance and strategic instincts, the necessity of their creativity, resonated with my gay sensibility. I had never seen a film that exploded so unreservedly with queer life as *Paris Is Burning*. It was a revelation to me. And, for the first time, I felt that I had found the community I'd been searching for, even if it only existed within the parameters of my twenty-inch television screen.

In the cast's refusal to dim their queer lights, I found my battle cry. Growing up, I had felt like a reject, the "gay guy," dismissed like the lisping jack-in-the-box on the Island of Misfit Toys. But *Paris Is Burning* emboldened me. If the ball walkers of *Paris* could be unapologetically themselves, then I would follow suit. And I didn't need the straight world's permission to do it.

I was *Paris*'s student. Each time I watched the film, it was like being educated in a queer classroom that had never before been available to me. I memorized the ball scene's language: "shade," "fierce," "reading." I even quoted Venus, a trans woman featured in the documentary, in one of the stories I was working on.

I realize now that I had very little in common with the cast of *Paris*. Yes, we were queer, but these were racialized people whose struggles had been insurmountable compared with mine, though back then I didn't quite see it that way. At a time in my life when I was searching for community and purpose, and trying to stand strong in my convictions, I saw only other queer people.

Through *Paris*, I felt I'd finally found my gay home.

A year later, I ended up moving to Toronto. I'd come to the realization that the life I thought I wanted, this comfortable backdrop, was ultimately getting me nowhere. If I was going to carve out a career for myself as a writer, whatever that looked like, I'd have a better chance of doing that in a larger city where more opportunities were available.

Not that the transition was easy. It was a shock, to move from that WASPy manicured city to the stained-sidewalk grittiness of Toronto. I was completely unprepared for Big City Life. I remember the first time someone asked me for spare change.

"Sure, okay," I said, reaching into my pocket. I had no idea I'd be asked for the same by someone else a few blocks later. And the block after that.

Toronto was a much more diverse setting than what I'd been used to, and the people I met, the symphony of languages I heard around me, the various ethnic neighbourhoods I visited, were exciting. And while I was intimidated, the energy of the city fuelled the budding writer within me. A whole new world was waiting to be captured in my stories.

It was also exhilarating to be part of a larger, and more eclectic, queer community, one that drew hundreds of thousands of people into the city's downtown core every June as part of its annual Pride Day celebrations. I recall watching all the people march past me at my first Toronto Pride parade, and how empowered I felt. Queer people truly were everywhere. And I remember marvelling that, although we may have looked different on the outside, we were all united in our fight for equality and rights.

Many years later, I had a very different experience at the Pride parade. There I was, standing alongside my partner on the crowded sidewalk, beneath the glare of an unforgiving midday sun, cursing myself for not wearing sunscreen. Or a hat. But at least I had on my good sunglasses, a necessary accessory for any self-respecting homosexual. As you get older, your attitudes towards Pride Day can change. It can cease being the party it once was. In fact, it's easier to see Pride Day as a growing annoyance. The crowds, the drunk people, the oiled models in corporate-coloured Speedos. And yet, for me, that's what also made Pride Day a source of endearment. It was a nostalgic experience, allowing me to mark my evolution as a gay man by reflecting on all the Prides of my past and the person I'd been then. And it was still nice to watch the parade, to see all those smiling faces, young and old, from all walks of life, and be reminded of the breadth of the queer community.

But that year, 2016, it wasn't the queer community that held my attention. It was a straight man. Specifically, Prime Minister Justin Trudeau, who was walking in the parade for the first time since taking office. After seeing him so many times on television, and in the shirtless pics that had found their way online, I was anxious to see how he compared in the flesh.

But before he could make his way to where we were standing, the parade came to a grinding halt. The participants in front of us, who moments earlier had been joyously waving their rainbow flags and blowing their whistles, were now left to just stand there, awkwardly fidgeting. The sight made me consider how much of a parade's enchantment comes from its movement, the momentum of forward motion and energy, the passing revelry.

"This is the worst-organized Pride parade ever," I grumbled to my partner.

We overheard someone say Justin was just a few blocks away. Was he as attractive in real life? I wondered. And was he wearing a shirt? I had to find out. So we waited, sweating it out.

Then a plume of purple smoke suddenly arose not far from where we stood, and I immediately became alarmed. Throughout all the Pride parades I've attended over the years, I've always feared that the parade would be a target for violence.

"I think we should go," I said, and my partner readily agreed. We made our way through the confused crowds towards the subway station.

Once we got home and turned on the news, we found out Black Lives Matter–Toronto had staged a protest during the parade. According to a spokesperson, the group was protesting the marginalization of Black, Indigenous, and racialized queer and trans people by Pride Toronto, the presence of police floats in the parade, and the lack of representation of queer and trans people of colour on the Pride Committee, among other concerns.

"Well, you fucking ruined Pride," I thought. I was angered by what I perceived as a colossally inconvenient and manipulative display. It stood in direct contrast to everything I believed Pride Day represented. Wasn't the parade, at its core, a celebration of inclusivity? And I never even got to see Justin Trudeau.

But the events of that day, as well as the news articles I read and the conversations that were sparked, stayed with me in the weeks that followed as I learned more about the reasons for the protest. About the way Black people were treated by the police, the racism that people of colour face on a daily basis, the threat of violence and discrimination experienced by trans people, and especially trans people of colour.

"You don't do something like that," a straight white woman had angrily said to me about the protest. "Not at Pride."

Not at Pride? Who was this person to tell me, a gay man, what was acceptable behaviour at Pride? Had she even been to the parade that year?

Her words gnawed at me until I finally heard myself reflected in them. I thought about the anger I had felt at the protesters' actions that day. But wasn't that what Pride Day had always been about—a protest? A demand for visibility and equality? And who was I to question what trans and queer people of colour had to say about their lived experiences? Who was I, a white gay man, to tell anyone what they should or shouldn't be doing at Pride?

I realized, Glen, with no small amount of irony, that the comfort zone I had sought to escape all those years ago had been replaced with another comfort zone, one of my own creation. I wanted a nostalgic Pride parade filled with floats and balloons and waving people wearing rainbow leis. The same unified parade that I had naively assumed I saw at my first Pride all those years ago.

While we should never take for granted the milestones we can celebrate as queer people, I understand now that the parade I saw back then had been viewed through a very narrow lens.

I returned to *Paris* recently. By that I mean the documentary. Over thirty years have passed since its release, and while it is still an iconic piece of cinema for many in the queer community, there have been numerous criticisms about the film over the years, including the fact that the filmmaker, Jennie Livingston, was white. I remember my surprise when I first found this out; I had never considered that the lens through which *Paris*'s cast was viewed had been a white one. Although, to be perfectly honest, I hadn't given much thought to the lens at all. Was the criticism of the role Livingston played in filtering (and exploiting) the lives featured in her documentary any different from the filter I felt straight people had cast over my gay writing? And although Livingston identified as queer, people have said it should have been a Black or Latino queer filmmaker at the helm of telling these stories.

You could argue that, without that white lens, *Paris Is Burning* might not have found its way to the film festival circuit or secured a distribution deal. And that's the shameful reality. (Another shameful reality is that the cast of *Paris* had to fight for what they felt was fair compensation for their participation in the film.) I'm grateful for what *Paris Is Burning* gave me as a young, gay white male at a point in my life when I was desperate for a sense of belonging and connection, but I've since come to understand that, in spite of those first impressions, *Paris* was never my home to claim. It makes me wonder: What Black or Latino filmmakers have been denied the opportunity to make a *Paris Is Burning* of their own? What stories by people of colour have never received the recognition they justly deserve? What queer audiences have never been given the chance to see their own complicated and fully realized lives on screen—in stories written by, directed by, and starring them?

But on this viewing, it was the loss that struck me most, specifically while watching Venus Xtravaganza light up the screen again, her vulnerability on full display, as she talked about the paths that she believed would make her dreams attainable. While the people in *Paris* were brave and resilient, they were constantly subjected to the inequity of the world outside of their balls. I realized, with a dawning clarity, how much I'd contributed to that landscape.

Venus was murdered when she was just twenty-three years old, two years before the release of *Paris Is Burning*. She was discovered under a hotel bed on Christmas Day. It was believed she had been there for four days. Her unclaimed body was about to be cremated before her house mother, Angie Xtravaganza, identified her. To this day, Venus's murder remains unsolved. The film brought her fame and legions of fans, but Venus wasn't alive to enjoy her newfound celebrity status. I wondered what, if anything, had changed in the three decades since the documentary came out, especially when violence against trans women of colour continues to be a constant threat. And I asked myself what I'd done to help end that violence.

I had worshipped Venus from the frame of my television screen, but I hadn't taken a single action to help prevent the murder of another trans woman of colour.

Glen, you likely know this yourself, but one of the biggest lessons in life is understanding that your own evolution never ends. Everything you've learned has to be relearned. Attitudes need to be constantly rechecked. Opinions demand to be questioned. In spite of what I thought I knew when I walked away from that university campus, my role as a student never ended. And while I am a product of my time, the city I grew up in, the school I went to, and the society that surrounded me, that doesn't mean I'm confined to it.

I was naive when I assumed being gay was my invitation to the ball. It wasn't. The colour of my skin afforded me privileges, enabling me to stand on the sidelines and watch a parade pass by, when there were so many other actions I could have been taking.

I'm just sorry I didn't stop to consider it before.

Sincerely,

Brian

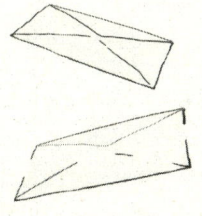

Letter 10

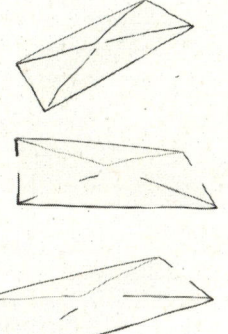

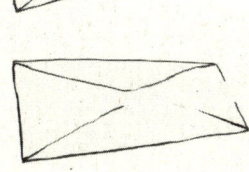

Dear "Student"

I am a university alumnus currently enjoying an early retirement. This has enabled me to pursue interests I could not while working. These interests include, but are not limited to: Philosophy, Ancient History, Politics and Music. I am well versed in numerous subjects. I am also a very good listener.

I am all too acquainted with the perils of the bar scene. The values it upholds are damaging to any meaningful relationship. The Lady Di's of this world are fascinating objects, but only from afar. As to the denim- and leather-clad citizens of the scene, I prefer to avoid them. Consequently, I come across as a well-educated, older gentleman who does not feel compelled to use the word "fuck" to make his points.

I would like to establish a relationship with a university student or a recent graduate. I too am tired of being alone. Physical endowments are one thing, but who one is, is far more important in the long run.

It pleases me to see that you have come to a similar
conclusion.

I would very much like to hear from you.
Should you wish to contact me, I may be reached at the
following telephone number. Ask for Randy M. That way,
I will know it is you who is calling. Should you get my
answering machine, simply leave a message that you are
wishing to speak to Randy M. and I will call back at
my earliest convenience.

I look forward to hearing from you. I remain

Yours truly,

Randy M.

P.S. By the way, I'm HIV negative.

Dear Randy M.,

Good lord.

You were a retiree and responding to the personal ad of a twenty-one-year-old university student. Cupid's arrow was pointed a little high, don't you think? Even the way you addressed me, "Dear 'Student.'" Come on. You have to admit that's pretty fucking creepy. And yes, I swear sometimes. Another reason it wouldn't have worked out between us.

I would have been open to meeting you, though. Just not for romance. I can safely say our stars weren't aligned for that. But maybe for a coffee. Or a glass of wine. I had a soft spot for older gay men when I was younger. I found them fascinating. I still do, even though someone will likely—and rightly—point out that I'm an older gay man myself these days. There's usually common ground to be explored between the different generations. The dance music, the camp, the humour, the same cultural touchstones—though I'm always interested to learn which touchstones have changed and which ones have held fast.

"What do you think of Madonna?" I'll ask younger gay men. (Apparently, not much.)

"When you hear nineties dance music, does it sound dated?"

"Do you know who Karen Black is?"

"Have you seen *Grey Gardens*?"

If I hadn't been so hell-bent on finding love, I would have liked to talk to you, Randy M. I would have been curious about your experiences. What were things like when you were twenty-one? And were you jealous of the freedoms my generation was enjoying?

That's one thing I've always wondered about—how the older generations feel about the liberties bestowed upon the younger gays. Marriage rights. Support groups out the wazoo. We even have our own Netflix category. Compared with how things used to be, even a few decades ago, queerness now seems like such an everyday presence. Not that prejudice and ignorance aren't a constant threat. Queer people still experience violence and discrimination on a daily basis, especially trans people and people of colour. For many, the fight for basic human rights is ongoing and unrelenting.

Still, did you wish you had what the younger generations have? Did you feel that a chunk of your gay life had slipped by, unlived? Because at times I've certainly felt that way. So many of my formative years were spent in darkness. And I'll never get those years back; they'll never be made right.

From when he was a young age, I suspected my nephew was gay. There were the same telltale signs that I recognized from my own childhood: a penchant for dolls, for dressing up. Even the same weight issues. And while I wanted to say something to him, I also knew it was his journey, not mine.

When he did come out at twenty, he'd had me as a role model his entire life, just by my honestly being who I am. What my nephew witnessed growing up was a gay uncle who was visible and accepted. I was always present, at every birthday party or Christmas Eve gathering, a gay family member, never pretending otherwise, never sitting in shrouded silence or awkwardly fielding questions about when I'd settle down with the right girl.

I never had that growing up. There were no openly gay relatives at our family functions, no same-sex spouses, no rainbow buttons on anyone's lapels. There was no guidebook to being gay, no road map. No examples of what a healthy and positive gay life could look like. Whatever path I walked down, I had to carve it out for myself, even if it felt like I was fumbling through thick brush most of the time.

If I'm going to be honest, I was a little jealous when my nephew came out. To my eyes, his coming out wasn't a big deal in my family because I had already done so much of the hard work. I'd already put in the time with my relatives. I'd had the uncomfortable conversations about how being gay was normal, how it wasn't a reflection of bad parenting skills, and no, nothing had happened to make me this way. (My mom had a theory that my homosexuality had been caused by a scare she got while she was pregnant with me while driving through the Rockies. This was also a woman who once proclaimed, "All gay men have thin fingers so they can do artistic things.")

But I was also proud of the role I had played in my nephew's coming out. I had helped make it a bit easier for him than it had been for me. And isn't that the point, Randy M.? Doesn't that make our struggle worth it?

Recently, I gave my nephew, now twenty-eight, and his new boyfriend a ride to a family function. It was the first time I'd met someone he was dating. Since he's come out, it's been fun having another gay in the family. We're not just uncle and nephew; we're gay uncle and gay nephew. And this means we have a bond, regardless of our age difference. We're by no means the same person, but there's an undercurrent of understanding between us, of our shared struggles and achievements, of the trajectory of our gay lives.

I was self-conscious about what his boyfriend might think of me. What had my nephew told him about me? Was I still relevant? Still hip? (The fact that I'm even using that word points to the obvious answer.) Even though there's often that common ground, in my experience, the younger generation can be dismissive of their gay elders. They rarely ask questions, and never seem all that interested in what I have to say. I'm not implying that I need the conversation to centre around me, but a few basics would be nice: What do you do? How long have you lived in Toronto? Who's your favourite queen from *RuPaul's Drag Race*?

This, thankfully, was one of several questions the boyfriend asked me. Leave it to drag queens to bridge the generational divide.

Needless to say, I saw potential.

This car ride made me realize how lucky the three of us were to be living openly as gay men. A few short generations ago, these drag-queen conversations wouldn't have happened. I might have assumed my role as the Closeted Uncle. I might even be married to a woman.

In spite of that luck, and the appreciation I felt while we debated the merits of Monét X Change versus Trinity the Tuck, that realization also terrified me. The freedom my nephew and I now enjoy hasn't been around for very long. Those broken lines in your rear-view mirror are never as far behind as you think.

But there we were, in that moment, driving along the 403, an uncle getting to know his nephew's new boyfriend for the first time.

It was a perfectly normal scene.

Before my mom married my dad, she dated someone for ten years who I'll call Johnny. Everyone in the family had heard about Johnny over the years. He was, by my mom's accounts, the most fascinating person she'd ever dated. (And my mom had dated a lot.) He'd been an entertainer, a singer and a dancer, and had even run his own dance studio.

"I used to play the records for him," my mom said proudly.

I'd seen photos of them together, her impossibly young face smiling back, complete with bumper bangs.

"I can't believe I was ever that thin," she'd sigh. "Those are my real teeth, but I had problems. I had them taken out after you were born. You took all my calcium, Brian."

Looking at the photos, it was obvious to me that Johnny was gay. The bleached-blond hair was a dead giveaway.

"Men didn't do those sorts of things in the fifties," my mom whispered to me once, as if we were standing at her locker between classes. "But Johnny didn't care. He got teased something terrible, though. The other boys would be after him constantly."

I wonder if a fixation with hair colour is another common denominator among gay men. I had an unfortunate Sun In Hair Lightener episode in Grade 8. I'd intended to bleach a single lock of my hair, like Andrew Ridgeley from Wham!, but coordination was never my strong point and I ended up spraying half my head. I went from brunette to strawberry blond in a matter of days. The teasing from my classmates was relentless. I patiently explained that I hadn't dyed my hair, I was using a new shampoo that accentuated my natural highlights, but no one believed me. My parents, who had also noticed, told me to stop or else people would think I was a fag.

I wince as I write that now. It's hard to believe they'd say something that harsh to me. But their words are immortalized in the journal I kept at the time.

Such was the taboo of a boy bleaching his hair in the mid-eighties. Imagine Johnny doing it thirty years earlier! The teasing would have been merciless. (It makes me wonder about the choices we make as queer people, especially in our adolescence. Did I really think I could somehow escape the teasing, that I'd be heralded instead of being reviled? Or was it one of those self-fulfilling prophecies— had I willingly courted the disapproval of others, and sealed my fate of being named the thing I dreaded more than any other?)

Johnny became part of my mom's—and our family's—folklore over the years. He was the showman of her past, the tap dancer she'd lost her heart to. How could she not have known? I wondered. How could she not have seen what was so obvious to everyone else?

When she was in her sixties, my mom and Johnny reconnected at their high school reunion. I'd been out to her for ten years by that point and was curious to learn more about him. My mom told me he was living in Las Vegas, in a mansion ("It's Diahann Carroll's old house!"), and had been with his partner for twenty years.

"He looks very good," she said, her voice still resonating with some of that teenage crush. "But I think he's had plastic surgery. His skin is awfully shiny."

A few years later, after my dad died, Johnny invited my mom to Vegas for a visit. She begged me to go with her.

"I'll be too nervous on my own. He knows you're gay. I'll even pay for your ticket."

I understood what this bright spot of excitement would mean to her, especially in the dark time following my dad's death, but I had mixed emotions. On the one hand, was there anything more anticlimactic than going to Las Vegas with your senior mother? But I was more than a little interested in finally meeting this larger-than-life character from her past. And I knew this reconciliation would give my mom some closure. There she was, bringing her gay son to meet her former gay boyfriend. It was practically a Hallmark movie in the making. Working title: *Gays of Our Lives*.

The good news was that Johnny and his partner were everything I wanted a pair of aging Las Vegas homosexuals to be. They greeted us at our hotel wearing silk shirts with loud, colourful patterns and were draped in so much jewellery I was surprised they could lift their heads and arms.

"Welcome to fabulous Las Vegas!" Johnny announced as he gave my mom a swallowing hug.

They had us over for dinner that first night. It wasn't quite the mansion my mom had described, but it was impressive enough. One of the rooms was plastered with framed black-and-white photos of Johnny and his famous friends over the years. He and his husband had even known Liberace.

Throughout our few days together, they showed us the sights. Johnny was boisterous, theatrical, and generous. I came to appreciate some of the spell he'd cast over my mom, the freedom he would have offered to a teenaged girl whose path in life, like many women of that time, had been predetermined.

We went out for dinner on the last night of our visit and Johnny told a few stories about my mom.

"We were at a party once and Doreen had a few too many drinks. She got up on a chair in front of everyone and started telling dirty jokes."

"Johnny!" my mom squealed. "Don't tell Brian that! Oh, I was so embarrassed afterwards. I felt just terrible."

It's easy to think of your parents as simply that: parents. That they came into being the day you were born. But they had lives before you, before your family, before they were married to one another. And that's one realization that's remained with me in the years since that trip. Johnny showed me a side of my mom I'd never known—a tipsy, teenaged girl in love, telling dirty jokes.

"Do you think it's possible a gay man can still love a woman?" my mom asked me on the plane ride back. "In a romantic way, I mean."

I said that anything was possible, but I held back what I really thought: Johnny was as gay as they got.

But to say that would have ended my mom's fantasy. And that's what I think Johnny had meant to her—an escape for the young girl with few options, and for the grieving widow looking for a respite from her sadness.

Later, I realized what it was I found interesting about older gay men like Johnny. They were a rarity.

I'm glad to hear you were HIV negative, Randy M. If you were a retiree in 1992, even an early retiree, it meant that you were likely among the generation hit hardest by AIDS. I came the generation after—I was one of the post-AIDS gays. By the time I entered university, in 1990, I knew what AIDS was. There was still stigma around the disease, and judgement and general bullshit. But at the very least, I knew how it was contracted and how to protect myself.

Condoms, condoms, condoms! That was drilled into my generation, gay and straight alike. You couldn't turn around without seeing a safe-sex poster staring back at you. There were even songs about it on the radio. People were making up for lost time, for ignoring the disease—and its earliest victims—for so long.

In my last year of university, I worked as a waiter in a restaurant that was down the street from my apartment, the one I moved into after sharing a house with my roommates.

My new apartment wasn't much to look at. It was tiny and tacked on to the side of an old house sandwiched between train tracks and a gravel parking lot. The bathroom was narrow like a bowling lane. And there were mice. I'd set out traps and then race to my bed, pulling the covers over my head, terrified I'd hear the snap. But the apartment was mine, and it was the first place I had ever lived alone, and the first place I had ever lived as my true self.

The restaurant was in a Victorian house, the kind you see in downtown areas that harken back to more charming and sophisticated times. I'm not sure when the house made the transition from residential to commercial, but I could only wonder at the number of restaurants that had blown through its doors over the years. I don't know what the owner knew about running a restaurant (and truthfully, it didn't seem like much), but because he was gay and well known in the community, the restaurant attracted a gay clientele. This is one experience I've never taken for granted—dining at a gay restaurant. It's so comforting to not be the only gay couple in a public place.

Many of the owner's friends would come in during the empty afternoons and sit at a table by the window, chatting, drinking coffee, and acting campy, the smoke from their cigarettes spiralling towards the ceiling. Maybe you were among them, Randy M. You would have been around the same age. Some of the men had AIDS. There was such a definitive look to the disease back then. The gauntness. The hard ledges of cheekbones and forehead. The shocking uniformity.

I remember sensing this instinctive internal shift whenever I saw a gay man with AIDS. A chasm was instantly created between us. He was over "there" and I was over "here," even though I might be standing right next to him. I suppose I could lie and say I felt compassion for these men. That I understood, so plainly and starkly, how easily it could have been me instead. It still could.

I did feel sympathy for them—how could I not? These men were being robbed of their lives—but I didn't feel compassion. I told myself that I was smarter than these men. Younger. Stronger. I was better. Because they had AIDS and I didn't.

Time changes you, as you likely know. I've become more aware of my vulnerability as the years have passed. And what those years have shown me is that the invincibility I once believed I'd earned was nothing more than an illusion. There was no force field surrounding me. True, I had a force field of knowledge, so that counted for something. But that knowledge wasn't my birthright. That force field wasn't protection I'd earned. If anything, despite that chasm I'd imagined between my younger self and those men in the restaurant, the only things separating us were luck and a handful of years.

I went back to that restaurant just last winter. I had returned to my university town for an extended period. My mom was in the hospital, dying, and my sisters and I were taking turns sitting at her bedside, waiting, as you do when someone is in palliative care. My mom slept mostly, but I still felt a compulsion to be there at all times. When I wasn't in the room with her, I'd worry about how she was doing, if she was in discomfort, if the orderlies had repositioned her or changed her, if the Daniel O'Donnell CD that we had on repeat had stopped and she was lying there, alone, in silence, which, to me, seemed the worst possible fate.

It almost became an addiction, this bedside sitting, even though there was nothing to do besides look out the window at the other hospital room windows or just stare at my mom, trying to imagine what life would be like without her, without her phone calls and the sound of her voice, which had been so much a part of my life's soundtrack.

I learned that this act of imagining a world without a loved one in it is called anticipatory grief—a way to prepare yourself for losing them. But you can't, of course. You can't really understand or feel the loss until it comes. And there's no way to gauge its impact, or how you'll reconcile yourself with that silence. How you'll process the memories at a later time, once there is no hospital and no bedside to sit at, once you attempt to return to some semblance of normalcy.

I needed to take breaks. I was wearing myself out. So one day, I decided to put aside my worries and take the day off. I never get to explore the city where I once lived as a student. My sisters and their families live there now, and it's always drive to this house, then drive to that house, then drive back to Toronto. All that sitting and talking and eating. And I never have the chance to simply walk around, alone, with no responsibilities or family obligations.

I revisited some of the places I used to go to when I was a student. Things change, but they also don't. It seems I'm always caught between the past and the present, comparing the two, trying to figure out how they intersect with one another.

I ended up walking to the restaurant where I had worked all those decades ago. That restaurant had been closed for years, and other restaurants had come and gone since then.

On that day, I saw there was a new restaurant at the location, a Tex-Mex place. And it was open. I hadn't been inside since I worked there, but it was lunchtime and I thought, "Oh, what the hell?" The waitress took me to a small booth, and after she left, I took a good look around. Needless to say, the decor was different. Sombreros and crucifixes on the walls, skeletons dangling from the chandeliers. But the overall layout was the same. It wasn't hard to imagine my younger self moving about the tables. Even the table by the window was still there. But it was empty.

I thought about how the men who once sat at that table are long gone. They've dissolved like smoke. I was still there, though, in that moment, a middle-aged man myself. Sitting at my booth for two, deciding which tacos to order, debating if I should tell the waitress about the connection I had to the place, if it would be worth the effort. It's always a risk, isn't it? To try to connect with a stranger. Sometimes it works, and sometimes it can make you feel even more alone.

After I was done my lunch, I went out into a bright and surprisingly balmy January day, the sun causing my eyes to squint. I walked further down the street, to my old apartment, which was still there. It looked rundown, faded, but there were still signs of life inside—blinds in the window, a few items propped up on the enclosed porch. I imagined another student was living there now. A gay student, who walked under the rail overpass every morning like I used to, taking the same path along the river to the university. I wondered about his life, the differences and similarities between us, both now and back when I'd lived there, almost thirty years earlier. Maybe he was fully out, and everyone in his life had known since he was a teenager. (Can you even imagine that possibility when we were that age, Randy M.? But it's true, kids are coming out younger and younger.) Maybe he was in love or healing a broken heart. Maybe he walked along that river every morning and took stock of all the undefined territory that lay before him. The promise and the possibility of the days ahead.

I thought about Johnny, who had died a few years earlier, from cancer. I thought about my young nephew, and the open path in front of him. I thought about my own life from where I stood, squarely between them both, and how the randomness of luck had spared us.

It was still early, and I didn't want to go back to the hospital just yet. I wanted to wrap this respite around me and delay my impending grief for as long as possible.

I considered what I wanted to do with the rest of my time.

Sincerely,

Brian

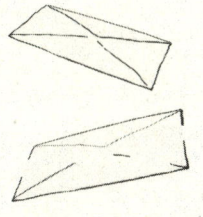

Letter 11

~

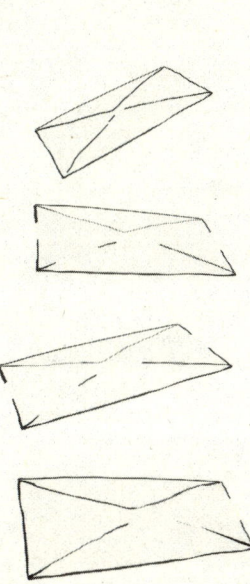

Princess or Rambo wannabe? Not this guy!

Friendly, 30 yr. old farmer, 140 lbs, 5'9".

Just a regular country boy tired of playing games and tired of spending his nights alone. Looking for a down to earth type. No head games, please. Into dancing, bars, fun. Easy going, reliable and looking for company. Where is every body? What more can

I say? Better stop now before I screw things up. Including my address and phone number, whichever you like. Home after 4:30 until about 7:00.

Hoping to hear from you.

Alan

Dear Alan,

I can't believe you gave me your address. Phone numbers were one thing, but addresses, Alan? With an invitation to drop by any time between four thirty and seven p.m.? I could never just throw the door wide open to a stranger like that. A *gay* stranger, nonetheless. I'd be a wreck, swivelling my head every time I heard a car turn down the side road.

Maybe life was like that in the country. No need to bother with calling ahead. No doors locked. Pie with a lattice crust and a full pot of coffee always waiting in every kitchen.

Or maybe it's that times have changed since you wrote me your letter.

Maybe it's me that's changed.

When I was growing up, having company was a big deal. My parents didn't entertain much and extended family visits were rare. My mom was a chronic worrier on the best of days, but entertaining, *hosting* people, would send her teetering on the edge. There was always so much to organize. The beach towels had to be removed from the sofa and armchair. The orange-and-gold shag carpet needed to be raked and vacuumed. The fake fur toilet tank cover, seat cover, and matching mat would be tossed into the washing machine. The kitchen floor might get a good scrubbing, even though no amount of Spic and Span could scour away the yellowed tinge of the linoleum. The basement, with its former living room furniture from the sixties, would get aired out and dusted. I'd even be forced to clean my room to give the impression that I was a well-behaved, orderly child who made my bed every day.

Whenever we were expecting company, I wouldn't be allowed to sit on the couch, speak to my mom, or touch any food. (Although I was a master at sneaking squares from Tupperware containers, rearranging them each time to make it appear as though none were missing.)

In those days, as you might recall, there were no cell phones. So the best any out-of-town company could say would be "We'll get there after one p.m." or "We'll be there around dinnertime." My mom would march back and forth from the kitchen to the living room window, wearing a trail on the carpet, checking for approaching cars. She'd have to prepare for the energy it took to entertain, to put on a revved-up, more animated, lipsticked version of herself, someone who acted as though we ate roast beef and scalloped potatoes every night.

Sometimes, out of boredom, I'd yell "They're heeeeeere!" when my mom had gone back to the kitchen, just to watch her come tearing back into the living room.

"Why did you do that?" she'd scold after seeing that I had lied. I'd usually get a swat from her tea towel before she went back to whatever it was she'd been doing. I'd wait another ten minutes before doing it again to the exact same results. It helped pass the time.

That was what life was like back then, in the seventies. Things were more loosely scheduled. Plans were vague. If you were late, you were late. You couldn't blame the traffic in a text. You probably wouldn't even stop at a payphone to call. Arrivals could happen any time within the span of three hours. Hotels were booked unseen. Phones would ring and you'd pick up without having any idea who would be on the other end. The doorbell would chime—and we wouldn't be filled with panic. There were also these things called phone books that were delivered free to every house in the city. Not only did they list your name and phone number, but also your address. Just imagine!

It feels like that's all changed now. Many of us have since grown afraid of the world. And afraid of other people. No knock is ever good news. No unrecognized phone number can ever bring a welcome greeting.

It was a different time back then, Alan. And the word that comes to mind is "open."

When I came out, I experienced a tsunami of emotions. All of the feelings that had been bottled up for twenty-some-odd years were finally unleashed. Much of it had to do with the fact that I was genuinely heartened. I'd been so certain I'd only be met with revulsion and rejection when people found out I was gay—that was, after all, the message I'd heard time and time again. But that wasn't what happened. And so I felt tender, raw, and filled with the amazement that comes when you break down a wall and emerge out the other side.

I wrote letters to my friends telling them that I loved them. I gave my sisters poetry for Christmas (even though one had asked for a hair dryer). I read the *Tao Te Ching*. I'd been in darkness for most of my life, but now I had stepped forward into the light. I believed I had a gift to share.

Yet there's been a gradual change as I've aged. While I understand it's impossible to maintain periods of high emotional intensity—and wouldn't that make you the most annoying person in the world?—I feel that I've become more closed off as a person. I'm not as sincere as I used to be. I can't imagine writing poetry for anyone or telling a friend that I loved them.

I don't dislike people. But I've grown tired. It feels like I've built another wall, creating a barrier between myself and others. At the midpoint of my life, I can honestly say that I've made my world smaller, not larger.

I don't feel open anymore, Alan.

I remember having a conversation with a work colleague a few years back. We were discussing friendships and I told him I didn't need new friends. I think he was insulted (we later became good friends and he likes to throw my comment back at me every now and then), but what kind of person says something like that?

I don't need new friends.

As if friends were shoes.

What I meant is that new friendships take a lot of work. Cultivating them makes me feel like I have to package myself up in a certain way, force a bit of laughter, engage with others, pay attention to what they have to say. And all of that takes effort. So what I really meant to tell my co-worker was that I didn't have the energy to make new friends. I couldn't be bothered. And I didn't feel it was ultimately worth taking the chance.

A couple of years ago, I was visiting my mom at her retirement residence. She'd been living in the lap of luxury as far as she was concerned. She had her own one-bedroom apartment, meals that she'd rave about ("The roast beef is fork-tender!"), and new friends to socialize with. There was even a valet service for walkers. She'd been lucky to end up in a nice place.

"There are former vice-presidents here," she told me once. "Doctors. Educated people. Not like me."

This was one of my mom's vices, the feeling that she didn't measure up. She couldn't compete with what she perceived to be intelligent, higher-class people. She was afraid she'd say something stupid and people would look down on her. But my mom was also eminently likeable. She had an endearing, girlish sweetness about her and she was always the quickest to laugh at herself. She found her currency not in her brains but in her charm. She took care of her appearance, especially after moving into the residence. Every closet in her apartment was crammed with patterned blouses and coordinating slacks. She wore silver rings on most of her fingers, always had makeup on, and took pride in her cloud-white hair, which she had washed and set every other week. I think she enjoyed having a reason to get dressed up. The dining room, the social ceremony of it, motivated her to make an effort.

During this visit, I asked my mom to tell me a story about when I was a boy. I'd been having a hard time connecting to myself as a child, understanding the thoughts and actions of the gap-toothed boy who smiled back from class pictures. I wanted my mom to tell me something about myself I hadn't heard before.

"Honestly, Brian," she sighed. "Who can remember that far back? Before I forget, can you add honey to my shopping list? I like it on my Cheerios."

Naturally, I was annoyed. A mother not being able to recall a single story about her child? But I shouldn't have been surprised. My mom was someone who very much lived in the present: what she ate that day ("The cook is putting a new spice in the food and I don't care for it. Everything tastes smoky"), the television shows she watched ("Why do people talk so fast all the time?"), what she needed in the way of groceries ("That grain cereal keeps me regular"). All the minor details that filled her life and the space between us. Maybe life is like that at her age, I reasoned, even though I assumed the opposite would be true, that the past would saddle up alongside you. Old age was a time for reflection, for taking stock of your life, not providing a play-by-play of the egg salad sandwich you'd had for lunch.

But I was hurt that my mom couldn't remember a story about me and that she'd been so dismissive of my request. She hadn't even tried to think of a story. Whatever bridges she might have offered to connect me to the boy I was had crumbled away.

I felt like I had lost a piece of myself.

—

When my mom started to get sick, the change in her was heartbreaking. She stopped going to the dining room because she lacked the energy to make the journey down the hall. She had meals delivered to her room, but even then, she took only a few bites of this and that. There were no comments about fork-tender roast beef, no spice complaints. She'd had her hair cut short to make it easier to manage, an impulsive decision that she then regretted. She lost weight and was growing increasingly unstable on her feet. It became clear that her days at the retirement residence, a place she'd loved so much, were coming to an end.

One afternoon during this time, the two of us were sitting in her living room, she in her burgundy power lift recliner, which, truth be told, had been her real home for the past few weeks. I'd been shocked by the sight of her when I arrived. She looked mannish with her short, flattened hair, along with her bare lips, the pants she had trouble keeping up.

I suggested that she might want to call some of her friends, the ones she'd grown up with. They had been friends for their entire lives, they'd even been each other's bridesmaids. I thought it would do her good to reach out to them, to reconnect and take her mind off her troubles. Behind my words was the implication that she should tell them that she was ill. I didn't think it was fair for them to find out after the fact. I brought out her address book, all the names, addresses, and phone numbers written in that perfect cursive of women of her generation.

But she said no. She didn't feel like talking to anyone. She didn't want anyone to know that she was sick.

"I'd rather just watch TV," she said.

So I put the address book away, thinking of how all those phone numbers, those addresses, those names, were useless numbers and letters as far as she was concerned.

During a commercial, she said, "I don't enjoy anything anymore. My shows, my meals. I don't enjoy talking to people the same."

She didn't speak these words to me but rather to the room. To the furniture around her, the fake fireplace, the framed family photos that cluttered her shelves.

I've thought often about her words ever since. Do we close ourselves off as a means of protection, of preventing hurt or sadness? Does our address book remain shut because we see no point in opening it up? Do we will joy away? Or does joy slip away on its own, a column of sunlight on the wall fading to nothing, whether we want it to or not?

And I think about how much joy I've felt, or haven't felt, in recent years. And about the last time I poured my heart out to a friend. Or made small talk with a stranger. The last time I took a chance on something unknown, rather than staring at the ringing phone in my hand.

During the early days of the COVID-19 pandemic, some of my high school friends and I were texting pictures back and forth the old-fashioned way, by taking a photo on our phones of an actual photograph. I don't see these friends often. Not that there's not a desire to see them, but we're no longer a constant presence in each other's daily lives like we used to be. I was caught off guard by some of the shots of me. I had no memory of them being taken. It was a reminder that there were all sorts of pictures of me that I've never seen and may never see. When I saw these photos, it was like reorienting myself to a room I hadn't been in for years. That ugly suede vest with the fringe! What was going on with my eyebrows? And did I always have that many pimples or had it just been a bad week?

I never knew what would come through next in our text exchange, what random moment, remembered or not, would suddenly appear on my phone's screen. I came to understand how there were pieces of me, of my past, that other people held. And in seeing these photos, I realized how much I needed my friends, their snapshots, their memories, in order to complete the picture of myself.

As much as I value these friendships, some of which date back to my elementary school days, I also recognized how random their formation was. If I hadn't struck up a conversation with that person. If we hadn't been sitting next to each other in class. If I hadn't started working at that job, I wouldn't have this person in my life. You could argue that, eventually, we all find the friends we're meant to have. But that would mean you could just sit around and wait for everyone to show up.

It implies you don't have to make an effort.

I was with my mom in palliative care on my birthday. For the first year ever, there had been no gifts or cake or birthday kisses from my mom. She'd been in and out of consciousness, delusional from pain medication, and I decided I wouldn't mention it. I didn't want to upset her or make her feel guilty for forgetting. But in the end I couldn't resist saying something. I suppose, in some ways, I still needed that acknowledgement from her.

"You were in a hospital forty-nine years ago this very day," I said.

Do you know the feeling of being looked at but not seen? That was how I felt being with my mom at the hospital. It was as though she was viewing everything, and everyone, through a sort of haze. But in that moment, I watched as her eyes sharpened into focus. It seemed as though she suddenly took control of her body again. She made a sound, a soft exclaim, then a kissing motion with her lips as she reached out her arms to me. There I was, Alan, a crying middle-aged man, leaning over for a last birthday kiss from his mom.

Her gift to me that day was the piece of myself I'd asked for.

I'm not a closed-off person; the years have just worn me down a bit. The shop doesn't open as often as it used to, but it's important for me to throw open the doors every now and then, to reach out to the people I love, and to invite a stranger in, spark a conversation, be a little less cautious. Make the effort.

I wonder what would have happened, Alan, if I'd taken you up on your offer. Just shown up at your farmhouse without notice. Let's say around six p.m. You'd be coming in from a day in the fields and see a car turning into your driveway and you'd wonder, as your eyes squinted against the setting sun, "Now whose shitty car is that?" And I'd step out of

Mr. Feces, a nervous smile on my face and a small bouquet of flowers wrapped in crinkly plastic in my hand. (Would a bouquet be too much? Maybe a plant instead. A crocus.)

"Can I help you?" you'd call out. Your first instinct would be that I must be lost. Or that I was a salesperson. But then you'd see my Doc Martens, my ripped jeans, the crocus. The shirt I bought with my Bay card, especially for this occasion, which I'd be returning the next day. Then you'd realize who I must be.

Maybe you'd invite me in, apologizing for the mess. Farmhouses are hard to keep clean. The outside is always coming inside. Flies, mud, the smell of damp fields.

"I would've tidied up," you'd say. "Had I known."

I'd apologize, say that I should have called first. But you'd say, no, no, not to worry. You were happy I came.

"I could use the company," you'd say.

"Me too," I'd say, struck by the realization of just how much I meant it. How much I missed unplanned visits, and the curiosity that a car turning into your driveway awakens. The beauty in taking chances. Talking to strangers, Alan. Answering the door.

"Do you like pie?" you'd ask, and before I could even reply, you'd be taking a pair of plates down from the cupboard.

Sincerely,

Brian

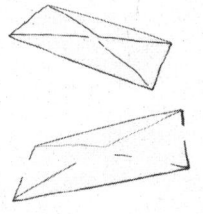

Letter 12

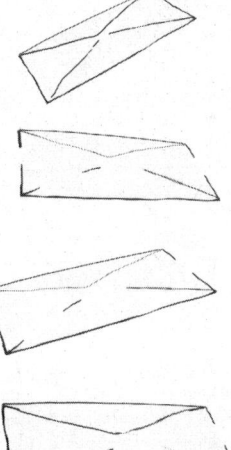

September 25, 1992

Hello.

I was reading the newspaper at work today
and saw your ad. It's one of the most original
ads I've seen in quite a while. I've placed
some ads but never had much luck. Answered
a few too but about the same. But something
about your ad seemed different so I thought
why not give it a shot?

We have some things in common. Like you I'm
tired of being alone. Bars are no place to
meet anyone for anything serious. Don't get me
wrong, I enjoy a fun night out but I don't go
out much. It's not much fun when you're on your
own. I'm not a Princess Di or Rambo wannabe
either. I'm an honest person looking for
someone who is the same. Anything worthwhile
has to start out as friendship but most people
won't give you the chance. They only have one
thing on their minds.

Don't get me wrong, sex is great and all,
but there's more to life than one-night stands.
I've had a couple of long-term relationships
but it's been a while since my last one, mostly
because it's hard finding someone looking for
anything serious.

A little more about myself. I'm not sure how
big of a deal age is to you. You said "same."
Well, I'm 34, black hair, green eyes, 5'10",
195 pounds.

I'm interested in cooking, dogs, plants,
hanging out with friends and spending quiet
nights at home with someone special. I smoke
and drink but only on weekends.

I'm not sure what else to write. Hopefully,
you're interested. Take a chance. You never
know. Even if we become friends or who knows.

                    Take care,

                        Liam

Dear Liam,

Your age was a definite deal-breaker. Thirty-four, to my twenty-one-year-old eyes, was ancient. In my mind, you would have carried a staff and had a long, flowing beard and your balls would have smelled like piss.

Am I exaggerating? Maybe a tad. But you were completely out of the range of acceptable ages. Thirty-four was *old*. Way older than it seems now. In fact, as I write this, I'm fifty, sixteen years older than you were when you wrote your letter. I don't imagine most twenty-one-year-olds would even consider replying to me. I'd be perceived as a lecherous senior. A writeoff. Something that lives under a bridge.

When did this happen? When did I paddle across to the other side of Lake Aged?

Looking back, I think of my early twenties as my blender years—everything was swirling chaos. Between the ages of nineteen and twenty-five, I lived in nine different places in four cities. I couldn't remember my own postal code at any given time. I had worked as a waiter, a server at two private clubs, an ad salesperson for a coupon clipper, a barista (although it was just called coffee shop server back then), a not-very-busy freelance copywriter, and even a travelling salesman. I had also traded in Mr. Feces for a sporty car that

I couldn't afford. It had a CD player that would only work when the heater was cranked full blast for at least thirty minutes. Imagine the agony I went through in July just to listen to Ace of Base! The car payments were $240 a month and I could barely scrape that together, let alone insurance, rent, groceries, and other necessities like cigarettes.

But I had youth on my side. And that counted for something, right?

What do you think your best years were, Liam? It's easy for me to assume mine were my early twenties, in spite of the disruption and uncertainty, in spite of all those postal codes and financial struggles. After all, I had youth, my dreams, determination, and stamina. But in retrospect, youth was never an accomplishment. It was a given. In fact, it wasn't until I hit my forties that I felt I was in my prime. I was stable in my career, I was in a solid relationship, and I had my confidence. Plus, I'd learned to say goodbye to drama and bad decisions.

I distinctly recall a moment in my early forties. I was getting ready to go to a birthday party and I checked my reflection in the bathroom mirror and thought, "This is the best you've looked and it's the best you're ever going to look."

I don't know how true that statement was. Was it *really* the best I've ever looked? Even better than the time I wore my burgundy blazer to the bar that one Saturday night? I'm sure there were lots of other times I looked better than I did at that moment. But maybe not. Some of us are late bloomers. We're the people who didn't peak in high school but instead bided our time and then blossomed when we least expected it. I certainly couldn't have predicted that bathroom revelation twenty years earlier. I wouldn't have thought it was possible I could look my best in my forties. I mean, that was *old*. But I did. Or at least, I thought I did. And I'm glad I had that moment in the mirror because there was a second half to that realization, which turned out to be true as well.

I've never looked better since.

I'm not complaining. It's just that, as I age, it's becoming harder to deny the inevitable. When the crow's feet started to appear in my mid-thirties, I remember thinking, "It's all over now. Time is creeping across my face." Not that I was serious. The lines weren't that deep, so it was still something to joke about, like your first grey pube. But at some point the crow's feet stopped being a joke. Because they deepened and were now accompanied by a waddle under my chin. Creases across my forehead. A neck that reminded me of raw chicken skin. These days, if I don't keep my hands moisturized, they look like jerky. I buy stupidly expensive creams and exfoliants, not because I'm certain they work, but because I'm too afraid *not* to use them.

When my last novel came out, I had a launch party. A couple of the people who came asked if they could take a selfie with me, and my first thought was, "Hell, no." But of course I said yes, because I'd make things worse by saying no. And then I saw the photos posted on social media. Why is it that the person taking the selfie always looks so much better than the person they're taking the selfie with?

It's not that I miss my youth so much as I don't enjoy getting older. I don't like the doubts it creates, the worry about selfies. I thought I'd be more carefree by now, but I'm not.

I'm too concerned about how my age defines me in the eyes of others, especially in the gay community, where beauty and youth can be king—or, as it were, queen.

I find myself asking, When am I too old for something? When am I too old to go to the bars? Too old to get drunk on a Saturday night? Too old to wear a certain article of clothing? (Not that I ever looked good in daisy dukes.) The other day, I stopped in front of the mirror before leaving the house and took inventory of what I had on: a faded pair of jeans, a Club Monaco sweatshirt, and a pair of sneakers. Was there really anything different about what I was wearing compared with what I wore thirty years ago? Even the knapsack I slipped over my shoulders as I made my way out the door was similar to the one I carried around in high school, only now, instead of textbooks, it was packed with work documents, my laptop, a Tupperware container filled with cut-up vegetables. At least my diet has improved. I haven't eaten a large bag of Cool Ranch Doritos for dinner in I don't know how long.

But as I waited for the bus, I started to question how I might appear to others. A teenager could be wearing the exact same outfit as me. Would someone think I wasn't dressing appropriately for my age?

I wasn't trying to dress young, I reminded myself. I didn't choose clothing based on what I assumed a seventeen-year-old would wear. The thought hadn't even crossed my mind. And, if we're really going to break it down, what today's youth are wearing isn't much different than what I wore at their age. The same ripped jeans, the same windbreakers and Converse sneakers. So who really has the rightful claim to these clothes?

Of course all these arguments reside in my head. I've never been stopped by a teenager on the street and accused of wearing something age-inappropriate. I've never been laughed at for my clothing choices. (That I know of, anyway.) In fact, I'm not even in their field of vision. I'm completely invisible to them. They couldn't care less what I have on.

That's the part that bothers me—I'll never be able to see myself as others see me, or size myself up in the same way. We all like to place one another in neat, tidy packages. That's more for our comfort than for anyone else's. Seeing someone in a different light implies our assessments might have been wrong. And people don't like being wrong. Especially, I'd venture to say, the younger gay generations. And especially when it comes to their opinions about us old fogeys.

There were two gay bars in the city where we lived in 1992, Liam. One, located downtown, was a dark shoebox with a DJ booth and a mirrored wall. It was the popular choice on Thursday and Friday nights. On Saturday nights, the other bar, which was located in an older residential area, was more popular. There was a pool table and couches and the beer was cheap. I suppose, technically, there was a third bar, located on the upper floor of the Saturday night bar. Not that my friends and I ever went to it, but we had to pass through on our way to the coat check. It was known as the bar where the seniors hung out. It was quieter. There were tables and chairs and lattice walls. A friend of mine from back in the day and I like to joke that if we were still living in that city, where would we be hanging out on Saturday nights—downstairs on the dance floor, or upstairs checking out all the young 'uns on their way to the coat check? Maybe we wouldn't be at the bar at all. We might be home, watching Lawrence Welk reruns in our pyjamas. It's hard to say.

Living in a mid-sized city, with an even smaller-sized gay community, it didn't take long for the bar scene to get boring or for faces to become familiar. Regardless of my boredom, I still felt compelled to go out to the same bars every weekend. It felt, at times, like an obsession. Miss one night and I'd risk the chance of not meeting that special someone. I wouldn't yet know his name or what he looked like, but I'd know it was magic the moment I laid eyes on him. And if I wasn't out at the bar, how could that moment happen?

Someone I'll call Tom was an older guy I'd see around at the bar. He owned a moving company, I think. He always made a point of coming over to my friends and me and chatting us up. We tolerated him because he'd often buy us beer. None of us were interested in Tom. We might have joked about him at the end of the night, as we sat in the parking lot eating late-night drive-through. I'm not kidding—I once had the capacity to eat a Whopper Jr. with cheese at two o'clock in the morning. These days, if I have a couple of Crispy Minis rice cakes at ten I wake up in the middle of the night with heartburn.

Once a month, the bar would host student nights, and it was such a relief to be with people our own age. To not have to put up with the Toms and their small talk or their hopes that, one of these nights, you'd mention that you often fantasized about doing it in the back of a cube van.

But Tom would always be at the bar, even at the student nights. I came to think of him as an intruder. A stain.

Lately, I've been thinking about how old Tom would have been back then. I'm guessing mid-thirties, but the canyon between us seemed much wider to my early-twenties eyes. Sometimes I see young men on the subway, or in the grocery store, and I hope for a glance back, an acknowledgement of attraction. I just want to know that I'm still on the radar.

It takes only a few seconds of me looking at a younger man to think about how I might appear to him. I forget how much older I am. I forget about the canyon. But then the subway passes through a tunnel and my reflection suddenly appears in the window and I see myself as he must see me.

Off the radar.

Maybe I was too hard on Tom. Maybe he was lonely and only wanted to talk. Maybe Tom forgot he was that much older than us. Or he simply didn't see himself the way that we saw him.

Maybe the Toms come back to bite us in the ass.

I hope you quit smoking, Liam. Take it from someone who's been around the block—that shit will kill you.

Sincerely,

Brian

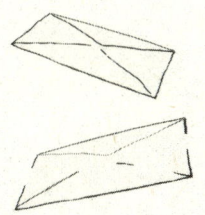

Letter 13

~

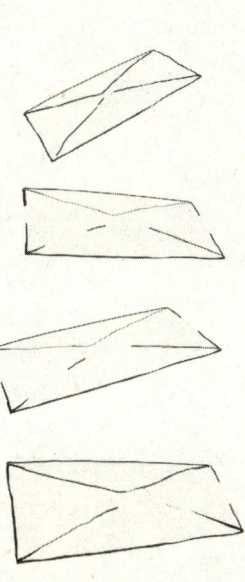

September 28

Hi!

Good news. I don't wear a tiara or carry a gun holster.
So hopefully that puts your mind at ease about the kind
of letter this will be.

Although I have self-confidence, I'm not like
Narcissus, either. (That Greek god who fell in love with
his own reflection.) I'm confident. But I'm not annoying
about it or anything.

So, university? Must be cool. After I graduate
Grade 13, I'm planning to go to university, too.
But not here, though. Unless you can change my mind.

Yes, I'm still in high school. I just turned 19.
So what if you're 21? I don't care. That probably means
you have more experience than me. Doesn't bother me
in the least.

In terms of what I value, friendship comes first. I
have to get to know someone really, really well before
things go any further. There's nothing I like more than
to just sit down and talk and talk and talk. And while

I'm a lot of things, boring is NOT one of them. When
you talk to people you find out their goals and dreams
and ambitions, which says a lot about who they are and
the things you can enjoy together in a relationship.
For me anyway.

I'd really like to talk and get to know you more.
I don't think you'd be dissapointed in getting to
know me, too.

One thing: is your discription in the ad (before
the "not") even close to the real you? Not that it's
important. I'm just curious if you did that to get
attention. You got mine, at least.

As to my physical discription, which I'm sure you're
not the least bit interested in... NOT! Ha ha. Okay, so
I've modelled in the past and hope to pursue a career in
it. In fact, I'm heading to L.A. next month to see if
I can get some work.

The compliments I receive, mainly from friends,
photographers or strangers passing by, mostly they're
about my hair, bone structure, my mouth and let's not
forget the almighty butt!! Not that I'm bragging or
anything. Also, I'm "straight" acting. Are you?

I live at home with my parents so giving out my
personal info is not an option. If you're interested
in meeting up, and I hope you are, I made up a code so
you can leave your phone number in the paper. I hope it
doesn't cost a fortune.

The code will be:

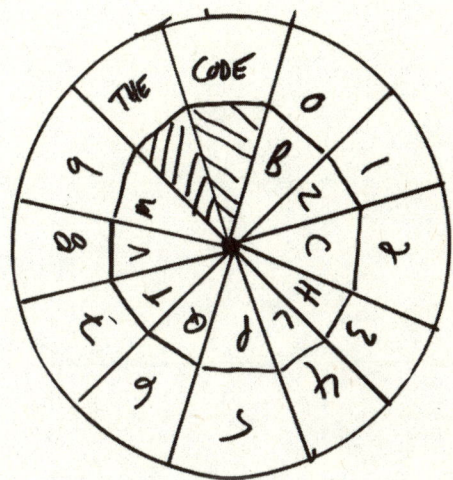

That means if you're number is 458-3349 (I just made that up), the code would be LPV-HHLM.

Amazing, right? I have a copy of the code, so I'll know the deal. As soon as I see your code, I'll call you right away.

I should let you get back to your studying. Please do the code thing. I'll be waiting.

It's been great writing you and I hope we can get together sometime. Even if it's just talking. The possibilities are endless! Take care of yourself.

Your friend:

Dear Indecipherable,

Just listen to the personality, confidence, and sass oozing from your letter. You were exactly the type of person I was hoping to meet. True, you were a little on the young side. And the reference to your almighty butt and potential L.A. modelling career *was* a bit cheesy. But your point was made. You got me.

Your method for responding, though. What was up with that code? Sure, I was desperate, but just how desperate did you think? You expected me to shell out more money, just to meet a nineteen-year-old with good bone structure?

I mean, *really*?

Okay, I did. Annoyed as I was, I couldn't resist the possibility of meeting you. There was so much promise in your letter. Yours, by far, was the best response I had received. Was my personal ad—and my sixty-five-dollar investment—about to pay off? Could it be possible? Had I found love through the classifieds? There was only one way to find out: I needed to place a second ad.

I did have some doubts. I worried that this was a scam, that you weren't real but were part of an organized crime operation that duped people into giving out their telephone numbers. What evil would I unleash as soon as I published my phone number in code? Or maybe you were a classified sales rep and this was part of a scheme to ensure lonely suckers like me kept pumping money into the newspaper.

Or maybe you were the Zodiac Killer. I mean, that code...

But to *not* do anything would have meant passing up on the chance of meeting you, passing up on a shot at love. And that was a chance I simply wasn't willing to take.

I couldn't remember, Indecipherable, what I'd said in my response ad to you, but I knew I had placed it. And so, as I did for my original ad, I went on the hunt twenty-nine years later to track down this piece of my past, too. Your letter was dated September 28, so I began looking for my ad in the papers published the week after, starting with the October 5 issue.

In case you're wondering how you go about finding a decades-old classified ad, it's not very glamorous. I spent hours facing a microfiche reader and scrolling through rolls of reproductions of newspapers, page by page. It was a painful, tedious process. Speed the microfiche up too quickly and I might whiz past a day's classified section— and my response—altogether. Go too slowly and I risked falling asleep in front of the machine and then waking up in a darkened, empty library basement at three a.m. with no hope of escape.

Once I scrolled through to the classified section of that day's newspaper, I needed to be on high alert. After all, I was looking for a single line in a sea of text, the tiniest string of words representing the hopes and fears of a twenty-one-year-old who, after years of hiding, had finally reached out. I wondered what he would have thought had he been told that his middle-aged self would one day be searching for his ad. If he would have understood the importance of it, what that time in his life would come to represent, and why it was so critical for his older self to find the ad.

It didn't take long for me to become familiar with the other classified ads published within the date range I was searching. This might sound strange, but I began to wonder about the people behind them. Did the person with the Bruce Springsteen tickets ever sell them? Did the unappreciated married man ever get laid?

These classifieds, long since forgotten in the dark isolation of their drawers, were now, miraculously, breathing again, brought to life against the glowing backdrop of the reader. Each of these ads had been in search of something, each had had a specific purpose, an end goal. Every now and then, I'd glance up and take inventory of the other people around me at their own readers. What were they looking for? I wondered. And were they having any luck?

What made my experience frustrating is that I couldn't find my ad. I checked the Companions column for October 5, 6, 7, 8, 9, 10, 12, 13, 14, 15, 16, 17, 19, 20, 21, 22, 23, 24, 26, 27, 28, 29, 30, and 31. Then I checked November 2, 3, 4, 5, 6, 7, 9, 10, 11, 12, 13, 14, 16, 17, 18, 19, 20, 21, 23, 24, 25, 26, 27, 28, and 30.

But there was nothing. Had I missed it? Did I need to start all over again? I considered walking away. Why did I need to find this stupid ad I was certain I had placed almost thirty years ago? What did it matter?

But if I couldn't find the ad, how could I be sure I had placed it? Maybe I'd been wrong and I hadn't responded to the letter at all. And if I'd misremembered that, what about all the other bits of my past—the pieces and swatches that I'd threaded together to make up who I was and what I believed? What if all the things I had assumed to be facts were simply not true? And what evidence did I have to prove otherwise? What if I couldn't prove my own life to myself?

In the late summer of 2019, I travelled to my hometown of Sarnia. I don't go back very often. I don't have much reason to, with no family and very few friends living there now, and nowhere to really visit except for the cemetery where my dad is buried. Even that seemed like a pointless destination at times, driving all that way to stand at a flat marker in the ground. I knew my dad would tell me not to bother.

"Save your gas, Brian," he'd say.

I had also planned to visit my mom. She was eighty-five years old, now living in the same city where I had gone to university, and she was waiting for test results. Her doctor thought she had lymphoma. My mom thought the doctor was full of beans. She believed doctors schemed with one another to send patients on endless rounds of specialty tests. That was how they made money, she theorized.

"I feel perfectly fine," she told me. "I eat good. I sleep good. My poops are normal."

My sisters and I knew she likely had cancer. The urgency of her tests seemed to affirm that. But she was convinced that the swollen gland in her neck was the result of the air conditioning blowing on a particular patch of skin while she sat in her power lift recliner, watching her morning talk shows.

"I put a towel on my neck now," she told me, as if that was the solution everyone had been looking for.

I don't believe in being the bearer of bad news, so I went along with my mom's theories. At some point, you have to stop reasoning with the elderly. It's too exhausting otherwise. And what was wrong with helping someone carve out some comfort? What was the harm of a drop of delusion in the onslaught of unrelenting reality? I'd been an expert at that, after all. I understood the importance, the necessity, of creating an inner alternate universe. Besides, nothing I could say would prevent her from having cancer.

"The towel might do the trick," I said.

"I think so," she replied with a nod.

I was going to visit so I could provide her with some distraction. We'd go to the shopping mall. Pick up a few things at the drugstore. She'd bring a handwritten list to be checked off as we made our way along the aisles: Kleenex. Hand soap. Polident. Afterwards, we'd go for dinner.

"My treat," she insisted. "I haven't taken my son out in a long time."

I told my mom I'd be at her retirement residence in the early afternoon. I hadn't told her about my plans to go to Sarnia in the morning. She would have questioned why or wanted to come along. She would have told me to go to the cemetery or to drive by our old house and report on whether the new owners were taking good care of it. Already I'd have obligations, and I didn't want obligations. I wanted the time for myself. I had already mapped out my route, planning to turn early off the 402 and then take Highway 22 the rest of the way, a stretch of asphalt that never seems to change, in spite of the years, with its farmhouses, abandoned gas stations, the flat concrete blocks that served as the only remnants of a motel that had once provided rest for people between their destinations.

It was August, and summer was winding down. The farmers' markets were filled with corn, cantaloupes, and tomatoes. The mornings were becoming greyer, the shadows longer. There's a beautiful finality about August, don't you think? All you can try to do is hold on to the pieces for as long as you can before they fade away.

As luck would have it, Highway 22 was closed for construction the day of my visit and I had to take the 402 all the way to Sarnia. I was disappointed, of course. Already the morning I'd planned so carefully was unravelling around me.

When I arrived in Sarnia, I drove around the residential streets. The familiar houses didn't look much different. Older, a little more slanted. Smaller. That's the feeling I always get when I'm back home. There's the version of your hometown that resides in your visual memory, the one that pops into your head in the course of a workday or that you conjure at night as you try to fall asleep, mapping out routes, testing yourself on the names of streets that were once as familiar to you as family. But the real, three-dimensional version never quite matches. Streets look tinier. Narrower. Everything feels more closed in. It's easy for me to feel like a stranger.

I visited the cemetery next. Correction: I stopped off at the dollar store first to buy a new arrangement of fake flowers. A word to the wise: Never get a marker with a vase. The imagined emptiness of that vase will haunt you, especially when you live three hours away. You'll see it in your mind, not only on spring days full of blossoms but also under the blanket of summer's humidity and the crisp rustlings of autumn afternoons and on numbing winter nights.

As expected, the flowers in the vase at my dad's marker had blown away. A year had already passed since my last visit. I stuck the new flowers inside and hoped they'd last longer. I stared down at the marker, at the letters of my dad's name, the numbers that signalled his birth and death.

It had been almost twenty years since he passed away from cancer. A brain tumour, at the age of seventy. I was thirty at the time, an adult in some ways, but still very much a child.

My dad had always been there as a protector, someone to rescue me when my car broke down on the 401 or to offer advice, even if I didn't always take it. And when it came time to help him, there was so little I could offer. All I could do was watch this man of precision, the man who had built the picket fence around our backyard, fall apart, piece by piece. First he lost the ability to speak. Then he lost his vision in one eye. Then the use of his one arm, followed by his leg. I saw the cruelty of his disease, its indifference. My dad hadn't deserved this. But the tumour didn't care about the kind of person he was, the fences he'd built in the name of protecting his children, or that he'd only retired from a lifetime of shift work just five years earlier.

What I'd witnessed of my father's decline reminded me of how insubstantial we are, these lives that we hold dear, the people we keep close. Our only armour is the refusal to forget what we've lost, to fight as hard as we can to never let those memories dissolve into the abyss.

After I left the cemetery, I drove downtown and parked my car. I went to the public library. I hadn't been there for years, not since the time of card catalogues and overhead light fixtures that reminded me of aluminum ice cube trays. The library had modernized, though, as it needed to. The card catalogues were gone, replaced with computers. A renovation of some kind was going on. A couple of fans were blowing cool air. I went to the children's area, which seemed, more or less, the same as I remembered. Then I went to the stacks to look for my novels. My second book was there, wrapped in plastic, looking faded and old. But not the first book, the one set in Sarnia. Maybe it had been checked out by a local queer youth, someone wanting to see their experiences in their hometown reflected. But maybe not. Sometimes, I feel that my books are considered smaller, or niche, because they explore the lives of gay characters and gay themes. I tell myself to not take this personally, that it's just my ego talking. Still, it's hard to shake the suspicion that my work gets minimized when placed alongside other books perceived to deal with broader and more important themes. But my book was old, I reminded myself as I left. Fifteen years had gone by since its publication. And, at some point, most books die.

After I left, I walked to the Eaton Centre, even though it hasn't been called that for years. It's since been renamed Bayside Centre, but I'll never think of it as that. I wanted to marvel at its vacancy again, its desertedness, like a scene from one of those zombie movies where everyone gets eaten except for a handful of tough-talking survivors. I used to love going to the Eaton Centre. There was a feeling to it, an allure of grandeur, that you didn't get at Lambton Mall, which was on the other side of the city, with its Woolco and Canadian Tire. The Eaton Centre represented sophistication. The possibility of a life larger than the one you were living.

I roamed around, trying to remember the sequence of the stores. There was the Thrifty's where I bought a pair of pleated jeans with pleather belt hoops and accents on the pockets. (It was a look that had its moment in the eighties.) The W.H. Smith store where I purchased joke books to memorize in an effort to keep my classmates from noticing that I was overweight. The Le Château where I'd purchased a black double-breasted suit, the same one I'd be crowned in as the runner-up prom king.

But none of those stores existed anymore, at least not in this mall. Their windows had been papered over, their interiors sealed off to my eyes.

A few relics were still standing, though. The big brass clock that wasn't working. The fountain, which, surprisingly, was. And as I walked along, I wondered what would eventually happen to the Eaton Centre. It would never be a mall again, that much was clear. Would it be torn down? Would it be replaced? Or would it be allowed to slowly decompose, like the *Titanic* at the bottom of the North Atlantic Ocean?

I walked around a little more, but I was losing time. I had to be at my mom's by one or else she'd start to worry. But there was just enough time for me to take the Indian Road overpass, to the pipeline where my dad had worked and where I had worked in the summers the years I was in university.

The land around the pumping station is dominated by massive drums filled with crude oil. It's a wonder to me that I used to climb to the top of these tanks, and sometimes down inside them when they were empty. Each tank had a floating roof, and to walk across that roof as it warbled and buckled under my workboots—the cold, enveloping darkness of the thick black liquid just a few feet beneath me— was unsettling.

There was no climbing up tanks that day, nor would I ever do that again. But I pulled my car over to take a few pictures. The oil drums, once pristine and gleaming white, were now showing signs of rust.

Before I could take any photos, a work truck pulled up and a man stepped out. It was someone I had known many years ago, someone who had worked with my dad. It took him a few seconds, but he recognized me, and we exchanged small talk through the chain-link fence between us. He told me he was going to retire. He had worked for the pipeline for forty years. Things were not the same, he said, referring, I suppose, to the rusted tanks.

He asked about my family. Then he asked about my writing. I told him my third book was coming out in another month, but that I was still working full-time. Writing hadn't been enough to earn a living.

"I think we all knew that," he said. "Even if you didn't."

The way he said it, it was as if he was continuing a conversation I hadn't been a part of. Had my dad discussed my writing with him? The likelihood of my not earning money? It made me feel stupid, as though my foolishness were laid out, exposed for anyone to peruse and reject, like items at a flea market.

It wasn't long before I was back on the highway, driving to my waiting mom, leaving that morning and all of its events, both random and not, behind. And yet, not behind. The morning was still there with me, in the car, and would stay with me, taking on a shape in the days ahead. I knew there was a good chance I'd likely forget this day entirely in a few years: the dollar-store flowers, my missing library book, the empty mall, my dad's co-worker, my embarrassment. I'd lose the memory of the day.

Unless, I thought. Unless I write it down.

There are very specific things that I remember from my childhood, isolated moments when no one was present except for me. I'm the lone keeper of those memories: Playing with my Star Wars figurines in elaborately planned-out plots that had nothing to do with outer space. The sound of my bedroom window fan on summer nights. The metallic smell of the furnace as the heat rolled up through the vents for the first time in the fall. My small silver Christmas tree with the blue mini lights that I set up in my bedroom during the holidays. I'd lie in my bed with all the other lights off, staring at it and thinking it was the most beautiful thing ever.

These are the memories that I hold inside. And now, I guess, they're extended to you, Indecipherable. But it's so hard to articulate the feelings that those memories conjure. They're so personal, shaped by my own life, by the purposes that they served and continue to serve. When I go, these solitary memories will go with me. I often think one of my final thoughts will be of that silver Christmas tree. That wouldn't be such a bad way to go, would it? Seeing those twinkling blue lights one last time before they turn off for good?

Yet it's the loss of the shared memories that bothers me most, especially when those memories involve people who are no longer here.

I remember my dad taking me into the backyard one night to look at the man in the moon. I remember, or I *think* I remember, the two of us on the back step and my dad kneeling behind me, his arm stretched out over my shoulder, finger pointing towards the moon. The moon was humongous in the sky and hovered brightly just above the feathery tops of the pine trees in our neighbour's yard.

I have the memory of a figure of a man wearing a hat and carrying a bucket, who appeared to be running. It was very clear to me that's what I saw, but that couldn't actually be possible, because a quick scan of the internet will show you what the man in the moon is supposed to look like. And it looks nothing like what I remember seeing that night.

So did I actually see what I remember seeing? Or did I make up something in the years since? Maybe I saw nothing that night. Maybe it was just a big moon—which it was. I do remember that. And you can't deny the presence of the moon.

What's significant about that night isn't the man in the moon or what I thought I saw. It's the memory of my dad pointing the moon out to me, the memory of that back doorstep, the shadowed fence posts surrounding our yard, the pine trees, the feeling of his body behind me.

This memory has become increasingly important to me in the years since my dad's death because I'm the only one left to remember it. If I forget, that memory will disappear forever. And my dad, there on that night, he will disappear, too. But if I keep that memory alive, if I keep conjuring it and thinking about that moon, I keep him alive.

I keep us together.

And maybe that's why I hang on to the physical objects that I do. The unflattering photographs. The buttons. The bits and pieces whose value is to be found not in what they are but in what they represent.

And maybe that's what these letters, my responses to these thirteen strangers, have really been about. If I take the time to record my life, to give it shape, I take back the memory. And all the things I feared I'd lost in my small life, I find again.

Would you believe I finally found the ad, Indecipherable? After two weeks of searching and eye strain, I came across it. My response to you, with my coded phone number, had run earlier than I initially thought and appeared the week before I started my search. It read:

To Whom It May Concern: LTC QMVV. Brian

I can't tell you what it meant to finally find the ad. It was evidence of my past. Of my life. I had gone on a mission to prove something, and there it was, undeniable, in grainy black letters against a glowing screen. Looking at that ad felt eerie, as though I'd been searching in dark waters, uncertain I'd ever find it, and then, suddenly, in the distance, I started to make out the shape of the bow, the rusting hull. Something that had been abandoned for all these years had now been reclaimed.

But what did it ultimately prove?

You never called. At least, not that I know of. Or maybe you did call and said you'd call back and never did. Or one of my roommates forgot to give me the message. These sorts of things happen even now. Who knows how much of our lives are decided by missed connections?

But your phone call wasn't the point. And I think I understand now why I held on to these letters from strangers and why I decided to answer them all these years later. You helped me reclaim the pieces of myself that I thought I had lost but were always here, just below the surface.

You and all the other men who wrote me letters gave me back the moon.

After I found my response to you, I marked down the date and wording on a scrap piece of paper. I wound the microfiche back into its roll, placed it inside its labelled box, and set it back into its sequence in the metal filing cabinet. I closed the drawer. It's still there and will be there long after I'm gone. This is comforting to me, even though no one will ever know what that ad meant or the story behind it.

There are things we hold on to and things we let go of, and there are details of our lives that have disappeared without our even realizing it. But that doesn't always mean those details are gone forever. Maybe they're just waiting to be taken out from their cardboard box. Maybe they're just waiting to be discovered again.

Sincerely,

Brian

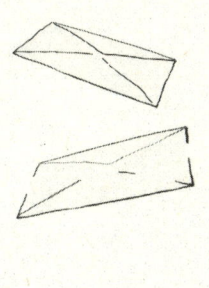

Letter 14

~

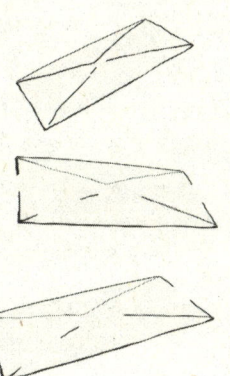

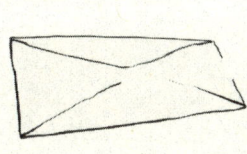

Dear Brian,

I'm writing to you from the year 2021. I know that must sound awfully futuristic, but you'll be surprised to hear I'm not wearing a silver pantsuit. Right now, I'm dressed in plaid pyjama bottoms and a T-shirt, sitting at the old dining room table that you refinished when you were a teenager. So even if you assume the future might be all lightboards and teleporting, it's not. There are still trees and apartment buildings and convenience stores. Still heartache and joy and people trying to make sense of their lives.

And yet, some pretty significant changes have happened to you. Before I get to that, I want to tell you a couple of things that should hopefully set your whirling mind at ease.

First, stop beating yourself up. Your inability to find the connection you're seeking isn't your fault. It isn't anyone else's fault, either. Mostly, it all comes down to timing. So please stop obsessing about your failure to find love. Have fun, relax, and make out with people. Those Saturday nights at the bar will remain some of your most magical memories, although they'll be harder to conjure in the years to come, and a little less vivid, too. Do us both a favour, will you? Put aside your romantic woes and self-absorption and try to be as present as possible on those nights. Stockpile as much as you can.

I know growing up gay in an unaccepting world has made you feel ashamed, fearful, and anxious. It has caused you to doubt yourself in so many unnecessary ways. I'm sorry that this has been your journey. You didn't deserve it and you're not to blame. (You might need to repeat this over and over to really let those words sink in.) But what I'm here to tell you is you will step out from those murky shadows and into light. Brilliance is on its way. It won't happen overnight and it won't completely cast aside those shadows, but they'll weaken. As I write this, at the old dining room table, the starless early morning has dissipated to an amber clarity. This is how it will be for you.

I'm going to give you a couple of dates. Mark them down and tuck them away somewhere safe, and when you feel the weight of those shadows, remember them.

MONDAY, JULY 19, 1993

This will be the day you come out to Mom and Dad. You'll be twenty-two and gearing up for your last year of university. You'll be living at home for the summer, working at the pipeline, in an ill-fated long-distance relationship (your first), and you'll be an absolute mess. By this point, everyone close to you will know you're gay, but word will start to spread beyond your immediate friends. You'll panic that Mom and Dad could find out from someone else. And you'll want to tell them so badly. When you're eating dinner, the words will be right there, a thorny ball on your tongue.

"Mom, Dad, I'm gay."

But you're never sure if the time is right, or if there ever will be a right time, so you swallow that ball back down, knowing that, as soon as you say the words, nothing will be over. Your journey with them will have just begun.

On this particular Monday, you call in sick to work. You won't be physically ill, but emotionally, you'll feel like you're teetering on the edge of a high diving board above a drained pool. Dad will go golfing late that morning and you'll be sitting in the den with Mom, you in the rocking chair. You'll notice a change in the air, a weightiness in the atmosphere.

"I think I know what's wrong," Mom will say, and you'll start rocking quickly.

"Mmm-hmm?" you say, trying to stall, already sensing what's about to come.

"Brian, are you gay?"

Before you can say anything, you start to sob. A lifetime of secrets and shame will surge to the surface. Years of excuses and guilt. The constant strain of your hiding.

You won't be able to speak, only nod.

"I knew it!" she'll wail. "I told your father, but he said I was being stupid. I knew I'd be dealing with this someday. That's why I watched *Oprah* when she had gays on."

She won't comfort you or tell you it's all right. She'll only be able to focus on what your revelation means to her. You see the wheels spinning in her head: What are the neighbours, her friends, the world at large going to think? She'll say that no one can know. Except, of course, your father.

"You'll have to tell him, Brian."

You feel a sense of inevitable dread. Coming out to Dad will mean confirming the worst: your failure to be the son he deserved. You know this news will only widen the gap between you. All you can do is keep rocking and wait.

Eventually the back door will open. You hear the clanging of Dad's golf clubs as he takes them downstairs. He has no idea what he's about to lose.

He'll come up the stairs, through the kitchen, to the living room, where you and Mom are sitting. He'll know immediately that something is up. Mom and her silence, not to mention your red-rimmed eyes, will signal that. He'll pause in the door frame, baseball cap slightly askew.

"What's going on?" he'll ask cautiously.

Before you can even open your mouth, Mom will open hers.

"I told you Brian was gay!"

And because your entire life has built up to this moment and you can't afford to screw this up, you'll look directly at Dad and say, "It's true. I'm gay. I've always known. Neither of you have done anything to cause this. It's just who I am. You've been a great father and I love you."

His reaction will be hard to gauge, as it always is with this man of action but so few words. He'll sit down in the armchair, fingers joisted across his stomach, and you'll wait, realizing that his opinion is the one that matters most.

"Well, if that's the way you are," he'll say matter-of-factly, "then that's the way you are. The love that was here before is still here."

You'll exhale, relieved, but still not quite believing his words. But for now, your secret is out. *You're* out. No more hiding and no more tears, for now anyway. You're too exhausted to feel much of anything.

You'll get up to go call your sisters, your boyfriend, your friends, to tell them the news. Dad will follow you out, and just as you're about to go downstairs to your room, you'll hear him say something to you. You won't catch it at first, it was just a tight mumble, so you'll turn and say, "Pardon?"

"I said I could give you a hug if you want."

Remember what I said earlier about being as present as possible? You won't realize it then, but Dad's hug will be one of the most healing moments in your life. So much hurt and pain melted away in that embrace. Years later, when he's no longer around to hug, you'll want this moment back more than anything.

In that hug, he put his picket fence around you.

There will be lots of conversations in the days, weeks, and months ahead, mainly led by Mom. She will go into a closet of her own. Both of them will experience some of what you experienced: the fear of judgement and blame, that they did something "wrong" in raising you, that our family is damaged. You'll understand their insecurity as parents, subject to everyone's opinions. Mom, especially. She'll need time to process this, to absolve herself of responsibility (this is when her "scare in the Rockies while pregnant" theory will surface), and it will feel like you're treading the same territory over and over again. Eventually they'll find their way through. Dad will write to his relatives in Saskatchewan to tell them. They'll help form Sarnia's first Parents and Friends of Lesbians and Gays—PFLAG—support group and answer the phone line to assist other parents in distress. Dad will march beside you in Sarnia's first Pride parade. They'll also come to Toronto Pride in 1996, along with your aunt and uncle from Saskatchewan. Mom will greet you and your new boyfriend in the lobby of the Howard Johnson hotel wearing a fuchsia pantsuit. "The gays love colour after all," she'll proclaim.

Dad will march with PFLAG in the parade. You'll think about the lie that the world told you and that you'd believed: that a father could never love or accept his gay son. But then a face you recognize will materialize in a sea of strangers. Your dad will walk past you, in his Tilley hat and clip-on sunglasses, surrounded by the applause and cheers of the crowd, carrying a sign that reads "We Love Our Kids." And while you'll feel gratitude and pride inside you, you'll also feel resentment and sorrow for all the silent years that passed between you and him, allowing the world to do all the talking when the only ones who should have been talking were the two of you. He'll die just five years later. Shortly before his death, he'll write in a journal that one of his regrets was not knowing about you sooner so that he could have given you the courage you needed. But you got that courage, Brian. It came just when you needed it most.

Years later, at Mom's funeral, a couple from the Sarnia PFLAG will come into the chapel and you'll start to cry as soon as you see them. PFLAG parents will always set off your waterworks. The fear of that parental rejection is still deeply rooted in you. But rejection wasn't your reality. It wasn't your story. There are times when you can hardly believe it yourself.

Time and time again, you'll be reminded that your experience isn't shared by everyone. You'll see first-hand the damage that parents cause when they turn their backs on their queer children, when they care more about the opinions of others than their child's happiness.

You were raised and loved by two good people. And for the rest of your days, this will be your anchor.

SATURDAY, APRIL 30, 2016

This will be your wedding day.

Yes, it will be a real marriage. In 2003, same-sex marriage will be legalized in Canada. And although your wedding date seems a long way off from 1992, twenty-four years from where you're currently sitting on your bed in the student house, marking your classified ad responses with *x*'s and *o*'s, the day of your marriage will actually be your twentieth anniversary. (He was the new boyfriend who met Mom in her fuchsia pantsuit.) Which also means that, as I write this in 2021, you're celebrating twenty-five years together. The good news is that silver is the traditional gift for a twenty-fifth anniversary. The bad news is that gold isn't until your fiftieth.

Okay, so no doubt you want to know more about your future husband. His name is Serge. You won't connect through a personal ad, but through a mutual friend. And, truth be told, this is one of the best ways to meet someone. His birthday will be two days after yours. He'll always hold the door open for you. He'll always say "bless you" whenever you sneeze. He'll always put cream in your coffee (although it will never be quite enough), and he'll always offer you the first bite of his chocolate bar, an act of selflessness that is incomprehensible to you. He'll like his gin martinis dry, three olives, and with just a spritz of vermouth. (Don't worry, you'll learn how to make them.) And, like Dad, he's a man of precision. He is a fantastic sewer. Your living room curtains will be testament to that. And talk about stylish! Everything Serge wears will be carefully considered, debated, then reconsidered. He'll spend hours shopping and come home empty-handed.

"I'm just so disappointed in everything," he'll sigh.

He'll support you unconditionally. Serge will be your biggest defender and never make you feel self-conscious for who you are. Being around him will feel completely natural. There will never be a day in all your years together when you haven't looked forward to coming home to him. You'll rarely argue and when you do, it will be about important things like whether the tomato knife should be used to cut anything but tomatoes.

You'll love him desperately, more than you're willing to admit or able to grasp. His presence will be so threaded throughout your own life, it will be impossible for you to imagine not hearing his voice come from another room or not folding his still-warm undershirts, not seeing his eyeglasses on the counter or his shoes in the foyer. Even in the middle of the night, you're certain a part of you can still perceive his presence, your slumbering bodies side by side.

Your years as a couple will blur together, but they'll have a way of sneaking up on you. One day, you'll note Serge's greying hair, a rounding in his posture. He'll see the same in you, and you'll see it yourself. You're a pair of middle-aged men now. You'll start to measure out your relationship in dogs. You've already had two; the second one is now fourteen. You'll no doubt get a third dog (Serge would be lost without one), but you'll also realize the next dog will likely be your last. And though you no longer worry about breaking up, the worry about a different sort of separation will begin to take shape. You won't dwell on it much; there are still many good years ahead for you both, fingers crossed. You want nothing more than to be two elderly geezers shuffling down the street, holding hands. But it's inevitable one of you will be left behind. Which of you will it be? And will the life that you once shared feel like it belongs to another dimension? Will the blur of all those years seem like the dissolving flashes of shooting stars?

One frosty night, when you're out celebrating your birthdays, you'll both remark that your twentieth anniversary is coming up.

"Maybe we should do something to commemorate it," you'll say.

"A party?" Serge will ask, likely already thinking about what he'll wear.

"How about a wedding?" you'll say, surprising yourself.

Marriage has always been in the background, but neither of you feel very strongly about it. After all these years, what would it prove? What would be the point when it's clear the two of you have already committed to each other? Besides, you've sat through enough weddings that seemed to be more about spectacle than about two people declaring their love for one another. But it's also true Serge and you have never done much to commemorate your relationship. And it would be nice, you'll reason, to bring everyone together, your family and all your friends, under one roof, and have a party. One thing you've learned, Brian, is that if you don't take the opportunity to pause and reflect, if you don't stop the frantic pace of your days to take inventory, life will sail past before you have a chance to pull the moments back.

When you tell people of your plans, some will ask why, after twenty years, you're getting married. The stress, the planning, not to mention the expense. But the answer will be clear to you.

"For the memory," you'll say.

While there will be details to sort out and agonize over in the weeks ahead (the guest list, the food, and the minefield that is the seating plan), your impending wedding will also cause some long-buried issues inside you to surface. You have never publicly declared your love for another man. You'll start to feel uneasy about the wedding kiss. It will mark the first time you've kissed Serge in front of your family and friends. The memories of those layers and layers of laughter from years ago, the punchlines, the revulsion, the seeds of rejection that were planted in a young boy, are still very much alive. And even though your family and friends all accept you, your hesitation about kissing your husband on your wedding day only highlights that a part of you still doesn't accept yourself.

When you confide your anxiousness to Serge, he'll say, "You're overthinking things. As usual."

He'll be right, of course. When you fixate on things to the point that you're not in the moment, you lose that moment. You tell yourself to stop listening to those voices from your past and instead focus on what's most important: the person standing in front of you.

Friends suggest you rehearse the kiss. But that doesn't seem like the solution. And you want that moment to feel authentic, not a performance. That kiss should feel as genuine as possible.

On the day of your wedding, just before the ceremony starts, you'll stand at the back of the room, taking in all your guests. Everyone you had once been afraid to tell you were gay will be there, joining in the celebration of two men in love: your mom, your sisters, your nieces and nephews, your in-laws, your friends from high school. Your university roommates, too.

And as the processional music starts and you make your way down the aisle, you'll realize this is what your wedding is really about: all the people you hold close, together in one room, for one moment. It will never be like this again. Even just a few years later, this same gathering won't be possible. Mom will have passed, as well as Serge's dad. And one of your university roommates. Another good friend, too. Life is fleeting, constantly spiralling into the past. And all we're ever able to hold on to is the precious present.

When it comes time for the kiss, you and Serge will lean in towards one another. It will be a bit awkward, but when is kissing in front of a crowd of people ever *not* awkward? As it turns out, the kiss itself won't be all that memorable. Nothing out of the ordinary. In fact, you'll hardly remember it.

What you *will* remember, in all the bright days and years ahead, is the chorus of cheers.

Love,
Brian

AUTHOR'S NOTE

As someone who is primarily a fiction writer, I'm always on the lookout for what I perceive to be fictional elements in works of non-fiction. What I mean is, when I read a story or book presented as "non-fiction," I find myself asking questions of the writer like, "How do you remember the sun was shining on that day in 1975?" Or, "How can you recall detailed conversations you had with someone twenty years after the fact when I can't recall what my husband said to me ten minutes ago?" (He'll no doubt claim I wasn't listening to him.)

The reverse is also true when I'm reading fiction. I'll wonder, What real events have found their way into the author's fictitious world? How often is a novelist drawing on the details of their own life, and the lives of others, to create their imagined landscapes?

Throughout the writing of this book, my memory has been stretched to its limits. I have tried, as best as I can, to capture various times in my life as precisely as possible. I've also resisted adding embellishments if I couldn't recall details with certainty. That said, memory is malleable and rarely perfect. And so even though this book reflects how I recall my life, there may be some unintended blurred boundaries between fiction and non-fiction within its pages.

With the exception of my parents and husband, the names and identifying characteristics of people mentioned throughout this book have been changed for reasons of privacy. With regards to the thirteen letters I received in response to my personal ad, I've done some rewriting. I've changed names, physical descriptions, and other identifying details in order to create new works. But I have tried to capture the unique spirit and personality of the original letters as closely as possible in order to maintain the creative springboard that inspired my replies.

ACKNOWLEDGEMENTS

Thank you to my editor, Anita Chong. You have supported this work from the very beginning and that has meant the world to me. Thank you for your precision, your honesty, and your talent. I'm coming away from our time together a more thoughtful and self-aware writer. That's a gift you've given me and one I'll hold close in the years to come.

Thank you to the McClelland & Stewart team: Jared Bland, Kimberlee Hesas, Sarah Howland, Lisa Jager, Erin Kelly, Shaun Oakey, Abdi Omer, and John Sweet.

Thank you to my agent, Dean Cooke, and to the team at CookeMcDermid.

Thank you to Rob Kempson for the vision, the leadership, the friendship, and the Arby's.

Thank you to Stacey Norton for all of your hard work and organization, and for your parents' mini lights.

Thank you to timeshare performance, Buddies in Bad Times Theatre, Summerworks Festival, foldA, the wonderful Kingston team, the Canada Council for the Arts, the Toronto Arts Council, and to the talents of: Colin Asuncion, Bilal Baig, Hume Baugh, Samson Bonkeabantu Brown, Keith Cole, Daniel Jelani Ellis, Izad Etemadi, Sandra Henderson,

Jeff Ho, Michael Hughes, Indrit Kasapi, Tsholo Visions Khalema, Brandon Kleiman, Daniel Krolik, Lucy McPhee, Eric Morin, Cossette Pin, Katie Saunoris, Adrian Shepherd-Gawinski, G. Kyle Shields, Katherine Smith, Chy Ryan Spain, Jonathan Tan, Curtis Te Brinke, Chris Tsujiuchi, and Geoffrey Whynot.

Thank you to Bill, Chris, Paul, and Andy.

Thank you to early readers Jamie Hunter and Tim McGregor.

Thank you to my parents, who are always with me, and to my family for their continued love and support. And to Ryan, Ella, and all the generations to follow.

Thank you to Serge, for every one of our memories.

Last, but not least, thank you to thirteen men who took a chance. I hope that love was waiting just around the corner.

LGBTQ2S+ RESOURCES

Even though it's been almost thirty years since I came out, the reality is that queer people today still face bigotry, ignorance, hatred, and acts of violence, especially queer people of colour and trans people. If you're struggling, help is available. Here are just a few resources.

TRANS LIFELINE

A national, trans-led organization dedicated to improving the quality of trans lives by responding to the critical needs of the community with direct service, material support, advocacy, and education for people of all ages. The hotline is run 24/7 by trans people for trans and questioning callers. Call 1-877-330-6366.

GENDER CREATIVE KIDS

A reference community organization that has supported trans, non-binary, and gender-fluid youth's affirmation within their families, schools, and communities since 2013. Visit gendercreativekids.com for more information.

THE LGBT YOUTH LINE

A service that offers confidential and non-judgemental peer support through their telephone, text, and chat services. Contact a peer support volunteer Sunday to Friday, 4 p.m. to 9:30 p.m. Call 1-800-268-9688 toll-free, text 647-694-4275, or go to youthline.ca to chat online.

PFLAG CANADA

Canada's only national LGBTQ2S+ organization offers peer-to-peer support striving to help all Canadians with issues of sexual orientation, gender identity, and gender expression. They support, educate, and provide resources to anyone with questions or concerns. Visit pflagcanada.ca for more information.

RAINBOW RAILROAD

An international charitable organization that assists queer people seeking safe haven from state-enabled violence, persecution, and the threat of death where homosexuality is criminalized. They provide information, connections, and funding for travel and other associated costs. Visit rainbow-railroad.org for more information.